Novel Writing *Mastery*

A Step-by-Step Guide from Concept to Publication

Tahlia Newland

ALKIRA
PUBLISHING

Novel Writing Mastery
Tahlia Newland
Copyright © 2025
Published by Alkira Publishing, Australia
ABN: 32736122056
http://www.alkirapublishing.com

Any reflections, descriptions or statements about real characters or events in this book are my personal opinion based on my own experiences.

ISBN: 978-1-922329-98-1

Contents

Introduction

I've always been an avid reader, and reading and writing do go together. As a teenager I enjoyed creative writing, and on my first visit to a careers advisor, I said I wanted to be a writer.

Her response was to suggest a field where I could find employment. 'So you want to be a journalist,' she said.

I shook my head. 'No, I want to write novels.'

'That's not a job,' she replied. 'It's something people do in their spare time.'

This conversation occurred sometime in the early 1970s, but it's essentially the same today. Some authors do manage to make writing their living, but most don't. Hobby authors' books, however, can be every bit as good as, and sometimes better than, any written by a career author. My editing career has been dedicated to teaching authors to write like pros.

But let's get back to New Zealand long before the advent of computers.

'You could be an editor,' the careers adviser added. 'Do an English Literature degree.'

I winced. I was looking for a creative job, and at that stage of my life, I thought editing was all about grammar, the purely technical side of editing. I didn't realise then that was only one facet of it, and more than four decades passed before I discovered that I had a unique talent for editing.

Like most authors, I followed a career path that had little to do with writing—though I did write scripts for the theatre-in-education shows I created and performed in for twenty years of my working life. I'd finished that phase of my life and returned to my first career—teaching—when the inspiration for a novel struck.

The day I decided to follow that inspiration and start writing *Lethal Inheritance* marked a major turning point in my life.

As a discerning reader, I had very high standards. Anything I wrote had to be as good as the books I bought at the store, like those by Cassandra Clare and Garth Nix, well-known talented authors in the young-adult genre of my first book. When I read over my first attempts, though, I was shocked at how far my work fell short of my expectations. The story appeared vibrantly in my head, but getting it onto the page in a way that did it justice was a skill I just didn't have at that time—at least not to the professional standard I expected of myself. Though I read many novels every month, I discovered that I didn't know anything about the craft of writing. So I had to learn to write, and later, because I wanted to know how to refine my writing, I learned to edit.

I was lucky in that I found excellent mentors, and writing advice was plentiful in my local library and on the web. My writing eventually earned me a literary agent, but I missed out on a publishing deal for my first book when the marketing department of Allen and Unwin (a major Australian publishing company) disagreed with the editor there who wanted to publish it. The marketing department thought it would be difficult to sell. Turns out they were right, but I had to publish and market it myself before I discovered that the metaphysical fantasy and magical realism genres that best fit my writing had only a small market. Still today, most people don't know what magical realism and metaphysical fiction are.

So though my hope of making money from the series wasn't realised, while working on it, I learned the craft of writing and editing. The finished product is, I believe, an outstanding psychospiritual work of fiction. It is important to me that I recognise the enormity of my achievement—the series is a vast vision, and brilliance is brilliance, be it recognised or not.

Because I didn't get a mainstream deal, I turned to self-publishing, and through that, I learned how to publish and market books. I made mistakes, of course, but because I learned from them, I'm now in a good position to help others.

I wrote many book reviews early in my literary career, and that led to people asking me to appraise their manuscripts. Authors returned to me time and again because they found my feedback insightful and helpful, and eventually one author asked me to edit his book. At first, I rejected the idea, thinking myself unqualified because I never did get that English Literature degree. But then I realised that such a degree, and even creative writing degrees, do not specifically teach one to edit. I had learned to edit from workshops, reading, practice and a very discerning eye applied to editing my own work. I also realised that editing was my favourite part of the writing process and that I would enjoy doing the same for other people's books. I obtained an editing qualification, became a freelance editor, and since then I have always had someone's book to edit.

The publishing side of my business began when one of my editing clients, who was frustrated with trying to find a publisher he could trust, said, 'Can't you publish my book?'

I realised that I could. And out of my desire to help authors avoid the sharks in the publishing industry, what is now called Alkira Publishing was born.

That careers adviser who suggested editing as a career likely noticed that my primary and high school reports always mentioned my exceptional ability for reading and comprehension. This is now known as hyperlexia, a neurodivergence which essentially means that my brain is wired in a way that predisposes me to excelling at decoding written language. This is no doubt why developmental and line editing are so very intuitive for me. Though I'm glad I followed all those other paths for employment in my life, I've now landed in a place that suits my unique talents perfectly. It just took me a while—and the arrival of the right technology—for me to discover that the careers adviser was right: editing is a good job for me.

Since beginning my editing career in 2012, I have helped countless authors to write and publish their books. I am dedicated to helping authors grow as writers and publish books of which they can be proud. Although many books on novel writing already exist, my skills and experience in working with all aspects of the writing and publishing process give me unique insights to add to the topic. I hope you find these insights helpful.

Tahlia Newland, June 2025.

How to Use This Book

This book is designed as a guide that you can return to repeatedly throughout your writing career. Early chapters outline the essential principles of the craft, and later chapters deepen them as your understanding and experience as a writer progresses.

Part One, Before You Start Writing, is full of personal advice stemming from my own writing journey and from my communications with my many editing clients. It's full of advice for those who are starting out on their journey or have started a book and are struggling to complete it. My aim is to help you gain the confidence you need to get started and overcome the kinds of obstacles and concerns that can keep us from fulfilling our desire to write a novel. This section includes advice on things such as determining whether your idea is worth pursuing, getting and keeping inspiration— something relevant to every writer. It ends with information on different genres—the single most important consideration when envisaging a book.

Part Two, Getting Started, covers the essential things we need to consider when we're ready to write our first draft. In it I outline the elements of basic writing craft and provide a basis for deepening the topics in Part Three. Topics include setting up a Word document for ease of navigation, point of view, plot and structure, outlining, worldbuilding, creating three-dimensional characters, writing a good opening paragraph, and tips on writing the first draft. This section gives you the information you need to get started with the elements in place to make the next steps smooth sailing.

Part Three, The Elements of Writing Craft, expands and deepens the topics presented in Part Two. Experienced authors could skip straight to this section to deepen their understanding of the craft. I've designed it to be studied *after* the completion of the first draft and in preparation for the revision process. I don't recommend this level of information for inexperienced authors who are about to write their first draft. Such detailed information could be overwhelming early in the novel-writing journey. It could result in overthinking, which can negatively impact creativity.

Consider this analogy: when you first learn

dance technique, there are a lot of details to remember and apply, and dancers who actively think about all the points of technique while trying to make up their own choreography tend to find their creativity compromised. But once they have familiarised themselves with the technique, their body falls into the correct posture without them thinking about it. Their creativity is then enhanced by correct technique, rather than being hampered by incomplete mastery of it.

So either get that first draft down before reading the detailed information on writing craft or give yourself several months to study and digest it before getting started on your novel. The point is that, for maximum creativity, you need to be able to write your first draft without actively thinking about the craft.

The last three sections can be read any time you want an overview of the full breadth of the novel-writing journey. Part Four covers the revision process, and Part Five covers editing. Both parts further deepen the subject matter of Part Three.

Part Six looks at publishing options and aims to help you make informed decisions about how to go about getting your book published. Part Seven gives key information on book promotion.

PART ONE:
BEFORE YOU START
WRITING

What Makes an Author?

When I began my journey as an author, I was very unsure of myself. I wondered if I had what it took and whether I could ever write a good book. I certainly didn't want to write a bad one! What I didn't realise at the time was that I already had the basic requirements—a love of books, a good imagination and a desire to learn. They're not enough by themselves to make an author, but they're what you need to start with, and if you don't already have them, you can develop them.

Reading Comes Before Writing

I still love picture books, and as a child, before I could read the words, the illustrations drew me into another world, the world of the imagination. A book was never far from my hands. I devoured them from the time I was very small. Nothing felt better than immersing myself in imaginary worlds that were so much more exciting than my own, and I soon found myself making up my own stories and play acting them out. Reading about other worlds was great, but so was making up my own world.

Through books I learned not only about different worlds but also, perhaps more importantly, about different people. I lived lives I could never have lived and met people I never would have met without reading. Books can educate and entertain, but they can also engender empathy in the reader, particularly for people unlike themselves.

This is a great grounding for an author. Reading gives you a wider range of experience to draw on in your writing than just your own life; it's as if you have lived all the lives of all the central characters in all the books you've read. A common suggestion for new authors is to write what you know, but if you read widely, you know about a great deal more than your own life.

It's Not Too Late

Even if the grounding of reading widely is not in your past, it is something you can do now. Ebooks are cheap and can be read anywhere, so really there is no excuse; just make sure that you choose good books. When I was a young adult, I read a series of depressing novels about boring characters who consistently made the most incredibly stupid decisions. I thought the books were dreadful, but they were highly critically acclaimed and had even won major Australian literary awards. I was so disgusted that this was what people considered great fiction that I stopped reading novels for about fifteen years. I read a huge amount of nonfiction during that time, but it was only when my daughter started reading the first *Harry Potter* book, and I decided I should read it too, that my love of fiction returned. Thanks, J.K.

Reading widely will not only help you decide on your genre, it can also help with other decisions as to how to approach your writing. For instance, when I considered writing the novel I had simmering away inside me, I wasn't sure if I should write in first person or third until I read *The Old Kingdom Series* by Garth Nix. Knowing which books are similar to your novel is also helpful when you come to pitch it to agents, publishers, reviewers or readers.

So if you want to write a novel, reading novels is the place to start, especially if you haven't read one for a while. And if you ask yourself why a novel holds your attention or why it doesn't, you can learn a lot.

Imagination

Reading is an imaginative pastime. The words tell the story, but the imagination is what brings it to life. When writing, I see the world of a story in my mind like a movie, and I become the characters living their story in their world. The unwritten scenes from my own novels invaded my imagination without permission and played out in full colour and sound until I wrote them down. Similarly, when I'm working on another author's book as their editor, I get inside the characters and immerse myself in their world.

If you experience the stories you read in this way, and if you find yourself dreaming up your own characters, worlds or stories, then you have a good imagination, a core requirement for anyone who wants to write a novel.

This kind of imagination can be developed by

imagining yourself as a character in a scene. Try to smell what they smell, see what they see, hear what they hear and feel what they feel. The more you can imagine yourself in the scene you're writing, the better your writing will be.

What makes the difference between a reader with imagination and a potential author is the desire to write their own stories.

Craftsmanship

Of course, we need more than a love of books, an active imagination and a desire to make our own stories to progress from being a potential author into an actual author; we also need to be enthusiastic about learning the craft of writing or, at the least, willing to learn.

I wrote the first draft of my first novel without having done any writing study, and that's fine because at the first-draft stage we don't need to concern ourselves with technique—the point is just to get the story down. When I realised that the novel wasn't very good, however, I felt miserable. Suddenly, the whole idea of writing a novel seemed daunting, and my confidence plummeted. I gave up the idea, but the characters and their story kept intruding on my mind. They demanded that their story be written.

So I decided to learn how to improve my writing—and you can do that too. Five years later, through intensive study, professional help and an unflagging commitment to my story, I'd turned that poor first draft into a quality product that an agent thought good enough to want to represent. The day I heard from that agent, I danced around and jumped up and down with happiness! The timing was right for that agent, but capturing her interest wasn't just luck; it was the result of my dedication to writing the best book I possibly could. I was ruthless in my criticism of my own work—a very good quality for an author to have.

If you're committed to excellence, and you're willing to learn and practise the craft of writing, you can write a good story—and this book can help you do it.

Inspiration

What turns a potential author into an actual author is studying writing craft *and* having the inspiration to write. Without inspiration, there is nothing to write, but with it, words will flow from your fingertips. If the inspiration is strong enough, as mine was, it will inspire all your study and keep you at the project until the end. The ability to keep the inspiration alive through many revisions and editing passes is an important quality—one that determines whether your desire to write will result in your eventually bringing a book to publishable standard.

If You Don't Have It, Develop It

If you don't already have a vast grounding in reading and using your imagination, and if you haven't already done some writing study and don't have any inspiration, don't despair; all these things can be developed. It's what we do now that will turn the potential author into an actual author.

I did it, and you can too. This book will help you get there.

If you don't have any inspiration but know you do want to write a novel one day, just keep reading, review the books you read, and study the craft of writing. One day the inspiration will come, and by the time it does, you'll be well prepared to take the idea and fly with it.

What I Learned from Reviewing (and You Can Too)

Taking the step from reading to evaluating what you read turns reading into a learning experience for the potential author, and the more you learn about writing, the better able you are to evaluate what you read. The better you are at evaluating others' books, the better you will be at evaluating your own books, particularly if you can differentiate between what you like and what is well crafted. Evaluating what you like is subjective, but we can approach evaluating good writing in a more objective way. And if you can develop a degree of objectivity in evaluating others' books, you can also apply that objectivity to evaluating your own books.

The ability to evaluate their own work objectively and in comparison to quality works in the same genre is enormously helpful for an author who wants to write a quality book. It's a skill well worth developing, and the process of considering what to write in a review (even if you don't publish that review) is an excellent way, and probably the fastest way, to develop the ability to evaluate your own work objectively.

I kept rewriting my first novel because I was able to be objective about what I'd written. I found it hard to admit that my writing was still not as good as the other books I read, but I was determined to write the best book I could, and so I did admit it. That, and the ability to stick at it until I was completely sure that my work stood up well alongside books such as the *Harry Potter* series, was what enabled me to get an agent for *Lethal Inheritance*. Had I not been so objective about my own work and so determined to produce a quality product, I would never have achieved that much.

The Part Application Plays in Learning

After beginning my study of the writing craft and writing the first few drafts of my first book, I wrote well over two hundred reviews in a couple of years. Through evaluating others' books, I became not only more objective about my own work but also familiar with the elements that made a well-crafted book.

Unless you consider and apply what you read or hear about a subject, you won't learn it very well. That's why courses involve exercises. Reviewing how well a book meets standards of craftsmanship helps you understand the craft of writing. Book reviewing is like an ongoing exercise for our writing study.

How to Approach Reviewing as a Learning Tool

No matter what you read, you probably have an opinion about it, even if it's just whether you like it or don't like it, but to help you learn the craft of writing, you need to be objective.

Even if you only consider why a novel works or why you couldn't read past Chapter Two, it will help you know what to do, and what not to do, in your own writing. It's good to read other readers' reviews as well, so if you see a lot of people complaining about cliffhangers or very short books, you'll know it's a good idea to avoid writing such books yourself. It's best not to annoy readers if you want them to read your next book.

But to evaluate craftsmanship, you need to have a clear idea of exactly what that entails, and the wonderful thing about coming up with a criterion for evaluation is that it gives you a list of the kinds of things you, as an author, need to study.

Criteria for Evaluation

Back in 2012, I set up the Awesome Indies Book Awards website (no longer operating) which gave Awesome Indies Badges of Approval to books that met the same standards of craftsmanship as mainstream books and Seals of Excellence for those we considered outstanding. I and a group of experienced reviewers with editing or formal writing qualifications set about evaluating not whether we liked a book but whether it was well written. To do this, we had to have a set of criteria on which to base our evaluations. The criteria listed the elements a book needs for it to be considered well written and engaging. I still use these criteria when evaluating if a book is good enough for Alkira Publishing, and you can use them to help you evaluate your own as well as others' books:

- The plot is well-structured, well-paced, conceptually sound and engaging.
- The characters are well-developed, and their dialogue and interactions with others are believable.
- The book is not overwritten or unnecessarily wordy; for instance; no obvious dumps of information, unnecessary repetition or irrelevant scenes.
- Changes in point of view are clear. No head hopping.
- The prose is well written and engaging. Where appropriate for the genre, voice and intention, the story is shown rather than told and the writing is active rather than passive.

Since we were evaluating published books, we also evaluated the editing, formatting and book-cover design, but the points listed are those that relate to the craft of writing.

To Publish or Not to Publish Reviews

Some authors do not want to appear critical of other authors' books, so there is no need to feel that you should publish your evaluations. You can simply do it as an exercise. Of course, a good review helps authors to sell their books, and it's nice to support authors whose work we consider good, but whether you publish your review or not is not important in terms of your learning. The process of evaluation is where the learning happens.

My book *The Elements of Active Prose: Writing Tips to Make Your Prose Shine* includes further tips for writing reviews and evaluating books.

What's Stopping You Writing That Novel?

Do you want to write a novel but haven't got started or haven't got very far before grinding to a halt? Considering how long it takes to write a novel, especially when you also have a job, it seems wise to start sooner rather than later, so what's stopping you? And how do you get over your obstacles?

I had an idea for my first novel for many years before I started writing—and when I did begin, I discovered that I had a series, not a single book! But what stopped me from beginning my novel was, more than anything, a lack of confidence in myself and in my idea. Only when I shared my idea with a publisher friend and she said she thought it was worth writing did I seriously consider going ahead with it, but I still faced the hurdle of not being sure if I could write a good book or not.

Lack Of Confidence

If I can do it, you can too. Why? Because I knew nothing about writing when I started, and I had no confidence, but I learned about writing, and my confidence grew from that. What I didn't realise then was that I did have the grounding an author needs—a love of books, a good imagination, and a desire to learn. Since you're reading this, you probably have it too, so allow that to give you confidence. It may not seem like much, but if you don't have those three things, writing is not the hobby for you. If you do have those qualities, along with an idea, then why not give it a whirl?

I didn't have writing skills, and that was a major cause of my lack of confidence, but I was willing to learn. If you really do want to write a good novel, and you're willing to study the craft of writing, you will eventually be able to write a decent novel, and your confidence will grow as you learn.

Of course, anyone can write a book, but not everyone can write a good book, at least not by themselves. With professional guidance, though, the likelihood of writing a quality book is greatly increased. I was lucky in that the right mentors turned up in my life at the right time. I had a beta reader who pulled me up on everything that didn't quite hang together and an editor who didn't miss a thing. And you can encourage your own team to do the same for you.

So don't think you can't do it, or even doubt yourself, or you'll never start. Instead, tell yourself you can do it. Say to yourself, 'If Tahlia wrote a novel before she knew anything about writing, then so can I.'

I even became an editor. Yes, it took many years, but I learned the necessary skills, and I loved every moment of the journey.

Say it now. 'I can write a novel. I do have what it takes.'

Think like that, and if you don't have what it takes now, you will develop it. Remember that we write a novel one step at a time, and the first draft doesn't require any writing skills apart from being able to use a computer and word processor (or pencil and paper). Truly, anyone with an idea and the desire to write it down can write a first draft.

Why You Might Have Stopped

If you've started and then stopped writing, it might be because you know, or someone has pointed out, that your story isn't working. Perhaps you have received feedback that makes you look at your story and think that you couldn't possibly fix all the problems. But with the right help and a good dose of determination, you can.

We are motivated by desire, and if our desire is strong enough, it will drive us to carry on. So if you feel unsure of your ability to finish a book, reaffirm your desire to do so. Remind yourself why you wanted to write it in the first place. In your imagination, enter your world and talk to your characters; I bet you love them, and I bet they want their story told!

And take it step by step. Get a manuscript appraisal, and if the editor you choose is good, they will break your tasks down into manageable steps. The *Novel Revision Checklist* you get if you sign up to my email list for authors will help too.

The Idea Is Too Vague

You may not have started on that novel, or you may have got stuck with it, because your idea was too vague. Mine was, at the beginning. All I knew was that I wanted the protagonist to climb a mountain and have to battle demons to get there. The idea was for the story to be a metaphor for the journey to spiritual accomplishment. My idea didn't flesh out until I began to write, but I did have a protagonist with an aim and antagonists who would try to stop her from achieving her aim. If you have these three things—protagonist, aim, and antagonist with a conflicting aim—you have the basis of a story. Your task then is to flesh it out.

So take your idea and make sure you have those basic plot elements, then in your imagination create your world and characters, enter that world and start writing. So long as you write while immersed in the world of your story and in the mind of your protagonist, the details will come to you as you write. Trust that.

Your first draft might be a mess, but that doesn't matter, because you'll shape it later.

You Don't Know How to Begin

Once I'd decided that I wanted to write my story, the reason I didn't start was because I didn't know how to begin. What I didn't realise at the time was that I needed to decide on something called 'point of view' (POV). The book *Sabriel* by Garth Nix showed me which point of view would work best for my purpose.

Point of view refers to whether you use 'I' (first-person point of view) when referring to your protagonist or 'he', 'she' and 'they' (third-person point of view). First person is the easiest and most personal, but it limits you to one point of view, unless you have different chapters narrated by different first-person characters. Using third person allows you to show the point of view of more than one character, and within that you can write as an omniscient narrator who knows everything or write in an intimate-third-person POV from the perspective of the character telling the story at any point. You need to decide on which point of view you'll be using before you can begin. See part two of this book for more detail on the different kinds of points of view. You'll also find the basic information on POV in my book *The Elements of Active Prose: Writing Tips to Make Your Prose Shine.*

Time Management

You have a day job, and maybe a family, so when do you write? The answer is when you are most likely to be inspired. Some write early in the morning. They get up at 5.30 am to write before going to work. Some write instead of watching television in the evening. Others write mornings in the weekend while their family is sleeping in. I sometimes wrote at 3 am because I woke with a scene in my head that I had to get down. I did suffer for it the next day, but if possible, write when the inspiration hits because that's when you will do your best writing.

However, if you don't have set times and wait for inspiration to hit before writing at all, you may not get very far. To get a book completed, authors usually have set times when they write, and they write whether they are inspired or not. I found that once I got started, the inspiration came.

Lack of Support

If you have a family, then you want their support, so talk to them about it. Tell them how important it is for you to write your novel, and ask them to help you by not interrupting during writing time and encouraging you when you're feeling down about your project. Your loved ones will likely support you if you ask for it.

Alternatively, don't tell them. At least then you won't get any discouragement! I didn't tell my family until I was well into the writing.

Have a question about writing? The internet has a wealth of information to support you. Just do a search. And there are countless writing courses and writers' groups you can join to get support. Also, a good editor will be supportive of your writing journey. It's never too early to run an idea by a professional.

The key to overcoming all obstacles is inspiration. At the age of fifty-two, I had such a strong idea that I simply had to write it down. I was so inspired that I wrote before work, after work, at lunchtimes and even sometimes in the middle of the night. If your inspiration is strong enough, you will find the time. But how do you get inspired and stay inspired? Read on.

How to Get Inspired and Stay Inspired

The key to overcoming the obstacles that stop you from writing a book, be it fiction or nonfiction, is to get inspired and stay inspired.

People tell me that one of my special skills is being able to inspire people, and I'm someone who never has writer's block, not once since I started writing solidly in 2007. I'm always inspired by something; it's my ability to bring things to fruition that is hardest for me. So do I have some tips? Yes, I do.

General Pointers for Inspiration

- Inspiration does not come to a mind that is trying to be inspired. If you're desperate to get inspiration, it probably won't come. Inspiration comes to a relaxed mind.
- Meditation will open your mind up to an uncluttered space where anything can pop up, but don't go for meditation that makes your mind dull and sleepy; go for awareness meditation that makes you feel clear minded.
- Inspiration usually comes to me when I'm doing something relaxing, like walking or sitting looking at a lovely view.
- If you're stuck, take a break. Giving up can be helpful—let everything go, and in the space you've opened, something new can arise.

If You Have No Idea What You Want to Write About

- Read books you like, not with the intention of copying anything and not with the idea of trying to find an idea, just to find the flavour of books you enjoy. You may finish a great book, and the next morning you wake up and the idea for your story is in your mind.

- Listen to music, close your eyes and allow images to come into your mind of a world that would suit the music, then populate that world with characters.
- Go to the theatre or the movies and imagine what a book on the same themes might look like.
- Sit in a café; watch people on the street and listen to people talking. Look at their faces, their clothes, their mannerisms and so on, and try to work out a back story for them.
- Ask yourself why you want to write something and allow that purpose to stimulate your mind into action.
- Visit an art gallery or photography gallery and look at portraits or pictures of people—or find images of people online. Find a picture you like and come up with names and backgrounds for the people in the picture. Ask yourself what aim the main character has and who or what would make realising their aim difficult. If you have these three things—a protagonist, an aim and an antagonist—you have the basis for a story.
- If you're visually minded, you could try creating a character with an AI art generator.

You Have an Idea, But You Can't Get Inspired

- Find music that suits the world and the characters. Select music for specific scenes. Listen to the music, and then once you're in the mood, write.
- Imagine your characters and have a chat with them. Ask them about themselves and get to know them. Ask what their hopes and fears are, and ask them to tell you their story.
- Do an image search for images that look like the setting of your story, and then practise writing descriptions of the settings.
- Imagine that you are in the story at whatever point you've got to; you are the character, and the events are happening to you. Ask yourself how you feel and what you would do next.
- Simplify your life. If you're too busy or too tired, you'll make it harder to find the inspiration to write.
- Try making a set time to write, a time when you're fresh, and write regardless of how you feel. Sometimes just getting started can get the inspiration going.
- Ask yourself why you want to write this story. Is your reason for wanting to write a strong

one? If it is, then focus on that and allow that reason to get you going. If you don't have a very strong reason to write this story, then see if you can find one. If you can't find that, then maybe this idea is not strong enough, and you should set it aside for a bit and allow other ideas to come up.

- Ask yourself if there are other reasons why you can't get started, something else that is blocking your inspiration.

- Sometimes we can't find the inspiration because we don't have the confidence that we have the skills needed to write well. In this case, studying the craft of writing can help. There are lots of options for ways to study—books, blog posts, workshops, short and long courses.

When It Gets Hard to Stay Inspired

Anyone who writes with the aim of getting published knows (or will soon learn) how much time and effort it takes to get a manuscript up to publishable standard. Every writer goes through many challenges and trials as they work on a book. Criticism and rejection are things we face many times during the journey, and if you really want to get published, you need to take criticism as a reason to improve your work, not as a reason to give up. In order to fix a book that's not working well, you have to find out what's wrong with it, and that means reaching out to someone who can help you.

Every book can be made better, even those already in print, so criticism doesn't mean your book is bad; it just means that it can be improved. My first novel took many years to write, during which time I did seven complete rewrites and twenty-seven edits.

How did I stick with it through all that? Didn't I get sick of it?

No.

Why?

It was satisfying to make my manuscript better: I would not look at it for long periods of time, anywhere from one to six months, and during that time I read a lot of quality books. It was easier to be objective after a break, and after comparing my book to the quality books I'd been reading, I saw quite clearly that it needed to be improved. At the beginning I wasn't sure how, but further study usually gave me an angle to take, and I found myself excited at the prospect of making it better. Each time I revised the book, I could see it was getting more and more like the book I'd imagined it could be.

I was learning all the time; I'd put so much effort into the book already that I figured that if I didn't make it even better, all that work would be wasted. Okay, not really wasted, but I thought I might as well keep learning and make it the best it could possibly be.

I believed the book was worth the effort. If you believe in the value of your book, you will stick at it. Maybe it's a story that needs to be told because it will raise awareness of an issue, or maybe you have something important that you want to express in your story, or maybe you just have a strong sense that the characters want their story told and you are their chosen scribe, or maybe you know in your guts that it's a great story, or perhaps you know people will find it really uplifting, or maybe writing a book is just something you've always wanted to do.

If you're not sure whether it's worth the effort, then ask yourself why you began writing it in the first place. Is that inspiration strong enough for you to keep going, or has it faded and become not so important to you now? Can you reawaken it? Has the story remained true to the original inspiration, or have you gone off somewhere and lost the driving force? If you've gone off somewhere, perhaps it's time to pull it back to the main point.

If you've lost inspiration entirely, revisit what got you started in the first place. The thing that kept me going more than anything with that first book was knowing that it dealt with something important.

I also believed in my ability to make the book better. I figured I should be able to learn how to write a good book, and I never stopped looking for ways to improve it. When I gave my first novel to my agent after editing it again in accordance with her suggestions, I really thought I couldn't do any better, but after a break and some further study, I discovered that I could.

I knew the downtimes would pass. Sometimes I felt that I would never be able to write well enough to achieve the kind of quality I wanted, and I'd feel depressed about the project for a while. That's natural, but I always knew that this was just a feeling and, like all feelings, it would pass. I knew that eventually I would feel more hopeful.

Giving up is most refreshing. Every now and then, I gave up. I decided it was all too hard and that it was time to stop. Then, with great relief, I would close my document and declare that I was finished with it for good. A few days or weeks later, however, I'd find myself back on the computer typing away. The break refreshed me, and that allowed new inspiration to enter.

What Does 'Write What You Know' Mean?

'Write what you know' is a common piece of advice you might hear about writing, but how valid is that proclamation? After all, did J K Rowling experience magic in her life? It isn't even real. All those fantasy, sci-fi and historical fiction books are not about our times or even our planet or realm, and yet authors write about them, so are they ignoring this advice? And have the authors who write about murders and describe the corpses actually walked onto a crime scene and seen a body like that? I doubt it. Certainly, some might, but plenty of others haven't.

What the Instruction to 'Write What You Know' Isn't Saying

'Write what you know' isn't suggesting that we should all stick to memoirs or contemporary fiction. It's not suggesting that a banker can't write about a scientist. It is, however, pointing out that it is more difficult to write about something you haven't experienced to some degree, and writing what you know is a very good place to start when you're a beginner writer. But the advice is still relevant for any author, no matter what their story; we just shouldn't take it at face value.

Many stories that have been written couldn't possibly have been experienced by the author, but an author with a good understanding of human nature knows about the most important aspect of any story—the characters. Even non-human characters work best when their interactions are aligned with human characteristics, reactions and modes of relating to other characters, objects and events.

The Benefit of Writing What You Know

It's easier to write about things that you know about than to write about things of which you have no personal experience.

- You are more likely to write with greater depth, understanding and clarity.
- You will be better able to accurately describe real places if you've been there—or at least watched a documentary about them.
- A personal perspective and writing that springs from one's experience creates a strong voice that resonates with readers.

Writing Your Life Into Someone Else's Story

Authors can draw on any and all of their life experiences and write them into someone else's story. Someone working in the pharmaceutical industry, for example, will become aware of issues in that industry, and these could become the basis for a story that examines those issues. Some authors set their stories in familiar work environments, where they know the dynamics. I'm not sure I could ever write about an office, for instance, because I've never worked in one! Reading books or watching movies set in an office would suffice to some degree, of course.

My life has gone through many changes, and each change brought challenges and experiences with it that I can draw on in my writing. I was a teacher who became a performer, then a teacher again, and then an author and editor. I used aspects of those life experiences in several books, but the character in the book experiencing those things was not me.

The *Diamond Peak* series has a parent and child relationship in it, and I drew on my own experience to make the dynamics of the relationship believable. I also wrote characters based on people I'd met and interacted with enough to get a sense of them and their life—at least to some degree. No character is ever based on any single person, but different characteristics of real people can combine into one 'hybrid' character. I have never done this consciously. It just happens.

Most of us have had some experience of romance, even if it failed miserably, so if you have a romantic thread in your book, look to your own experience for insight.

If you're looking for a weakness in a character, look at yourself. Maybe they can share one of your personal challenges, something you know about intimately.

Write What You Can Imagine Based on What You Know

Though my *Diamond Peak* series was set in a fantasy world where demons roamed, I spent so much time in that imaginative world that I came to know it intimately, and I spent so much time pretending to be my protagonists there that I really did come to know them well.

What if you are a woman writing from a male point of view or vice versa? Then you draw upon your own experience and observations of the opposite sex. If you're a woman writing a man, then watch men, listen to them talk, see how they react to their own life experiences, and read books written by men about men. The opposite applies to a man writing from a woman's point of view. If you know the opposite sex well, you can write as them well.

Learn About What You Don't Know

If there's something you want to write about but have no knowledge of, then you need to learn about it. Research is vital, and it's easy to do now that we have the internet. Want to write a historical novel? Then make sure that you study the time and the people on which your story is based until you know them well.

Want to write science fiction? Then study whatever area of science relates to your story.

Want to write about India or some other place you haven't been to? Take a trip before you start, and if you can't do that, then watch documentaries, look at photos and talk to people who have been there.

In *The Locksmith's Secret*, Ella went to England before I'd been there myself. After I'd researched and written the story, I sent the manuscript to a friend who had lived in England and asked her if it matched her impressions, and she added a few things that she thought the character might have noticed. When I arrived in London some time after I'd written the book, I found it exactly as I'd written it. I do have a good imagination, but it was the research that enabled me to imagine actually being there as the character. I also had plenty of other travel experiences to draw on for things like the plane trip from Australia to London.

The advice to 'write what you know' just means that you should draw on your own experience for your writing as much as possible, and that you should research any aspects of your story that you don't know well until you can write about them as if you know them personally.

Write What You Care About

One aspect of writing what you know is writing what you care about. Anything we care about, we're likely to know a bit about, and we'll also have the curiosity to do some research to find out more about the topic. Another good reason to write about things you care about is that you'll have a reason to write the book and a reason to finish it, and you'll be more likely to be able to maintain your inspiration through the challenges of writing a book.

What Keeps You Going

Writing a book takes a lot of time, and our life can easily take over our writing time so that the process becomes quite drawn out. Questioning our ideas and our capabilities are part of the process. Many authors, if not most, have times when they lose confidence in their book. Also, when we get to the stage where we need feedback, we may find that our work has a lot of problems. We may be faced with a rewrite so daunting that we wonder if it's worth it. And then there are the editing stages: first comes self-editing, which may have you wondering if you're doing it right, and then comes the professional edit. This will cost you money, so you may wonder if your book is worth the financial investment. How many authors give up before they get their book to a publishable stage?

The big question is, how do we keep our inspiration going in the face of these challenges? The answer is to write about something you care about, something you find important, something you feel people would benefit from thinking about. Fiction is a great way to examine issues and deliver information in a highly readable way—just never dump your information on your readers. If you include something you empathise with in your fiction, your book will be more likely to get to the publishing stage. Why? Because it's important to you; because you care about it.

Adding Depth

Writing about issues that are important to you will add depth that can turn an ordinary story into an extraordinary or important one. The depth of your concern will shine through, adding further layers and more complexity and interest.

You can add elements of what you care about to a story you already have, or you can write a story around something that matters to you. Either way, writing about what concerns you will make your project more important to you, and that will carry you through the tough times in the process of getting a book published.

What Do You Care About?

Ask yourself what you care about, and brainstorm a list of themes or issues, then see if one of the themes fits into your story somewhere or inspires a whole story. The easy way to add something you care about to a story is to have your protagonist care about the issue and the antagonist not give a damn.

The things you care about will likely appear in your writing to some degree or other anyway. Your job is to find them and draw them out.

I've always been concerned about bullying and abuse, and I've written two novels with bullying as the central theme, and one nonfiction work on spiritual abuse. The way the mind works is of interest to me, as are philosophical and scientific views on perception and the nature of existence. This interest area comes through in all my writing and adds to my unique voice. This gives me a sense that my books are important as inspiration and support for people facing difficulties. For me that makes them worth writing.

Voice

So let your areas of interest come through in your books. Don't be afraid to put yourself into your writing, because that is what will make it unique. With so many books out there, a strong, unique voice is more important than ever. Your passion for the things you care about will connect with readers in a way that the story wouldn't without it.

How to Weave It In

This doesn't mean that everything you write needs to be heavy with some issue—that can be very off-putting for readers—it just means that you should let what you care about come through into your writing in some way. Simply being aware of it can be enough; you don't have to have any particular intention to 'add it in'.

On the other hand, it can be a whole thread woven in around the central story, or it can be the main theme, or it can be something a character cares about enough that it has some relevance to the story.

Anything is possible. All you need to do is identify what concerns you and allow yourself to explore those themes or issues in your writing. The rest will sort itself out as you write or plan your story.

Why Are You Writing Your Book?

If a story has some importance for an author, they're more likely to stick with it. A story can be important to us simply because we think it's a great story, or because writing and publishing a book is on our bucket list. We might have a sense that our characters are demanding their story be told, or the world of our characters might simply be so strong that we can't get it out of our head until it's written. These are all reasons why writing a book might be important to us.

Write down somewhere the reason you're writing your book, and on those days when you're feeling as if the effort may not be worth it, remind yourself of that reason. If you still care about it, then you'll be more likely to keep working at it rather than giving up.

Is Your Idea Worth Writing?

Ideas are cheap, easy to come up with, but are they worth developing and turning into an actual product? This is the question that stumped me when I had an idea for my first novel. I didn't know if the idea was worth the effort it would take to write the book and finish it. Would the story work? Would anyone be interested in it? And did I have the skill to realise my vision for the book?

I believe that all ideas, with sufficient time, skill and commitment, have the potential to turn into a book worth reading, even if it is only for a small market, but some ideas will be easier to realise than others, and some ideas will be a lot easier to sell, so how do you know where your idea fits along this spectrum?

Time Commitment and Skill Level

The following categorisations are not in themselves indications of whether an idea is worth pursuing but rather indications of what you need in terms of time and commitment and skill level. These are just some of the things you'll want to consider when deciding whether or not to go ahead with an idea.

Ideas That Are Relatively Easy to Realise:

- Genre fiction set in our time and culture (no worldbuilding required), especially if the story is based on your own experience
- Ideas with a strong plotline—a protagonist with a clear goal and an antagonist with a clear reason to stop the protagonist from achieving their goal
- Fiction written in first person
- Fiction with one point-of-view character

Ideas That Take More Skill and Time to Realise Well:

- Fantasy fiction—worldbuilding and descriptive writing skills are required
- Mystery—police procedures need researching, and the plot needs lots of twists and surprises
- Historical fiction—needs research, worldbuilding and descriptive writing skills
- Anything involving a culture that is not your own—same as for historical fiction
- Stories written from a third-person-intimate point of view
- Stories with more than one point-of-view character

Ideas That Take Even More Skill and Time to Realise Well:

- Science fiction—requires scientific knowledge and worldbuilding skills
- Fiction without the usual protagonist/antagonist plot structure
- Fiction with deep conceptual, emotional, psychological, philosophical or issue-based themes
- Stories written in omniscient third person—

many beginners try to write in this form, but it takes considerable skill to make it engaging for modern readers

- Epic stories that span generations and involve complex politics and relationships

If your story fits the first category, then go for it. Simple stories can be powerful and very popular, and anything in the first category makes a good first book on which to hone your writing skills. Even if it never gets published, it's worth writing just as a learning experience. And if you're an experienced author, then such a book will be relatively quick and painless to write.

If your story fits the second category and also has a strong plotline, then it's also a good bet for an idea that is worth working on, especially if it's written in first person, but you will need to develop good descriptive writing and worldbuilding skills, and if you're writing in third person with more than one point-of-view character, you'll need to study how to change points of view smoothly.

If your story fits the third category and it's your first book, it might be a good idea to write a simpler book to start with. Many writing teachers suggest writing a practice novel, a novel that you write purely as an exercise while you study the craft of writing.

Of course, that's not what I did. The idea that inspired me fitted squarely into the third category. I didn't want to write anything else. And you might be the same, but that's okay, because if I, when a rank beginner, managed to realise my philosophical, epic fantasy to such a degree that it won awards, then so can others. It took me a lot of work, a lot of time and some financial investment, but I did it, and I now have a series of books that I am very proud of. I achieved my goal, and with the same kind of commitment, you can too.

Sales Considerations

If, when considering whether an idea is worth developing, we're looking at time spent in terms of potential financial return, then how well a book might sell is an important consideration. However, of all the people who write and publish books, only a small number earn enough to quit their day jobs, so I suggest that you think of your writing as a hobby. If it turns out to be more, great, but if you expect to become the next best-selling author, chances are you'll be disappointed, no matter how excellent your book.

Write because you love the craft and because

the idea in your imagination is so seductive that you simply must put it down on paper.

A golfer will spend a great deal on golf clubs and never expect to get that money back. Instead, they get the satisfaction of using a nice set of clubs and improving their game. In the same way, an author will spend money on editing for the satisfaction of creating a quality book. Sales are desirable, of course, but can never be guaranteed.

Popular genres such as thrillers, crime, mystery and romance are the easiest to sell because they have a big market. Fantasy and science fiction as general categories are also popular, but they have many subcategories, such as dystopian, paranormal, post-apocalyptic and so on that move in and out of popularity. Research best-selling genres to see what's selling well right now, and if your book idea fits into a popular genre, you can take that as an encouraging sign.

Publishers think in categories because readers tend to do the same thing. Any book that doesn't fit neatly into a category will be harder to sell than one that is clearly one thing or the other, unless you're aiming for the literary fiction market. Literary fiction is not as easy to sell as genre fiction, but that doesn't mean you shouldn't write it; it's just something you need to be aware of if you're to have realistic expectations.

Books in unusual genres such as metaphysical, visionary, magical realism, transrealist and so on are the hardest to sell, because these are niche markets. They have a small readership, and it's hard to get new readers for them as most readers don't even know what they are, let alone know whether or not they might like them. Your book might be very popular in one of these genres, but bear in mind that they are small, niche markets. My books fall into these categories, but I still wrote them.

Remember, however, that books in popular genres, though they may be the easiest to sell because there is a big market, are also in the areas where there is the most competition. There are large numbers of readers for popular genres, but to stand out from the crowd, your book needs to be of a high standard and well promoted.

Although you now may have a realistic idea of your time commitment and your book's sales potential, you still may not have decided if the book is worth writing or not. After all, my first series was the worst-case scenario in terms of time commitment, skill required and sales potential, and yet I still wrote the four *Diamond Peak* books. Why? I was simply really inspired. Was it worth it? Yes, without a doubt, but not in terms of money for time.

What made the time and effort worth it was that I gained a huge amount of satisfaction from creating a classic in metaphysical fantasy, and those books will remain after my death as a tribute to my vision and creativity—even if relatively few people have read them.

So this brings us back to inspiration and purpose. If your purpose in writing is to earn money, then the above factors are vital. However, if your purpose is to express yourself, then the only thing that really matters for deciding whether or not your idea is worth turning into a book is how inspired you are.

Inspiration Level

A quick quiz:
- Does your idea excite you?
- Do you get visual images of your story popping into your mind at all sorts of times?
- Do you think it's a great idea?
- Do your characters seem like real people to you?
- Do you love your central character?
- Does the topic have great personal meaning or significance for you?

The more times you say 'yes' in answer to those questions, the higher your inspiration level, and the higher your inspiration level, the more your answer to whether or not you should write your book is 'yes'.

Running It by Others—the Elevator Pitch

When trying to work out if your idea is worth developing or not, run the idea by other people. Tell them your idea and ask if they would read such a book. You'll need to condense your story into one or two sentences that present it well.

This brief summary of a book is called an elevator pitch because it's designed for an author to use when they're at a conference and they jump into an elevator with a publisher or agent. What are you going to say when you're standing next to someone who could put your book in every bookstore in the country? How are you going to sell them your book idea in just a few words? You can't give them a long, involved description; you have to say something that will grab them immediately.

If your elevator pitch grabs people, then it's definitely a story worth writing, and if you can write an interesting elevator pitch right at the beginning of your writing project, it will make the writing go more smoothly. I didn't do it for my first book until after I'd written several drafts, but once I'd done it, I wished I'd done it sooner. Writing my elevator pitch helped me to clarify what my story was about.

Genre

The first thing you need to decide when writing a novel is what genre it will be. It's the first thing a potential publisher or reader wants to know because it immediately gives them some idea of what sort of book it is. And it will immediately give you, as the author, some idea of what kind of story you'll be writing.

A book can belong to more than one genre, but it's advisable to have one main one so you have a clear marketing angle. Cross-genre and multi-genre writing is interesting, but for ease of selling, you need to be able to slot it into a broad category like contemporary or literary fiction.

Since this book is about writing a novel, I'll not be looking at nonfiction genres. In fiction there are two main categories: genre fiction (sometimes called commercial fiction) and literary fiction.

Literary Fiction

Literary fiction is more than just a book that crosses genres. To be called literary fiction, a book needs to go deeply into its themes and characters, the themes should be meaningful, and it should be moving and beautifully written.

Genre Fiction

The main genre fiction categories are:
- thrillers and mysteries
- speculative fiction (science fiction and fantasy)
- contemporary fiction
- historical fiction
- romance
- juvenile fiction (children's and young-adult stories)
- Secondary genres (that can combine with the main genres) are:
- horror
- metaphysical and visionary fiction
- magical realism
- coming of age
- women's fiction

The Main Fiction Genres and Their Characteristics

Thriller

The thriller genre generally has a fast-paced storyline imbued with tension and suspense from beginning to end. There are many subgenres within the thriller genre, such as the psychological, political and spy varieties. Some characteristics of the thriller genre include:
- suspense is incorporated throughout the novel
- plot twists to keep the readers guessing as they read
- the end of each chapter has a hook that encourages reading on
- high-action climax

Mystery

Mysteries focus on solving crimes and mysterious events. Ordinarily, the protagonist is a detective of some kind, and the remaining characters are suspects until proven otherwise. Common characteristics of the mystery genre include:
- a mysterious crime that needs to be solved

- suspects with motives that the detective must evaluate
- clues peppered throughout the work, including some that lead the reader to false conclusions
- a surprise ending

Science Fiction

Science fiction stories often take place in the future and involve fictional aspects of science and technology. Characteristics of science fiction include:
- space or time travel
- outer space or otherwise futuristic setting or alternate history
- advanced technology
- alternative social and political systems

Fantasy

Fantasy focuses on magical and supernatural elements that do not exist in our real world. They have action and adventure and often include elements of romance, mystery and suspense. Fantasy books typically include the following characteristics:
- magical elements and/or characters, like sorcerers, elves and witches

- conflict involving good versus evil
- imaginary worlds, often similar to medieval settings with high magic and low technology
- mythical creatures like dragons, werewolves or talking animals

Historical Fiction

Historical fiction is a story that takes readers to a particular time and place in the past, typically at least fifty years or more in order for it to be considered historical fiction. Although the story takes place in the past, it doesn't have to be one that actually happened in history. Authors can, however, choose historical figures, research their lives, and then write their story with the fictional elements being the parts of the story that were not documented.

Common characteristics of historical fiction include:

- a combination of historical and fictional elements
- a setting that exists in a historical time and place in the past
- themes common to the period

Contemporary Fiction

Contemporary fiction (sometimes called realistic fiction) is a story set in the present time or up to a few decades in the past. Contemporary fiction deals with themes of concern to modern readers and is usually more character-driven than action-driven stories. Characteristics of contemporary fiction include:

- conflicts that the reader could face in everyday life
- a setting that takes place in the present day and is an actual location or a fictional place that could be real
- characters that seem like actual people you might encounter in modern life
- conflicts that are solved in a realistic fashion

Romance

The romance genre can take place during any time and may contain a realistic plotline or have magical elements, but the primary element of a romance novel is that there is a central love story throughout the novel. Other characteristics include:

- two central characters who fall in love
- conflicts throughout the story that make it

difficult for the characters to be together
- a happy ending with the central characters together

Young Adult

Young-adult fiction is aimed at readers between the ages of twelve and eighteen. The plotline can be realistic or can contain magical elements, but in most young-adult fiction the protagonist faces challenges and changes that are relatable to an adolescent. Common elements in the young-adult fiction genre include:

- a teenage protagonist
- a love triangle in which the protagonist must choose between two potential love interests
- conflicts in the story that are age appropriate for the audience, such as trying to feel like they belong, succeeding in a sport or having a romantic relationship

Secondary Genres

Horror

The horror genre's purpose is to create feelings of terror and excitement in the reader. Common characteristics include:

- explorations of the darker aspects of humanity
- main characters whom readers can identify with and who often have haunted pasts and emotional traumas
- supernatural elements, such as ghosts or demonic forces
- a goal of provoking terror in their readers

Metaphysical and Visionary Fiction

Metaphysical fiction are stories with aspects that are beyond the normal, tangible world, usually spiritual and supernatural elements. Visionary fiction is usually the story of someone's spiritual awakening.

In metaphysical fiction, though the philosophy underlies the story, the story takes precedence over expression of the philosophy; in visionary fiction the expression of the philosophy may be more evident.

Magical Realism

Magical realism stories have a real-world setting along with magical elements, often blurring the lines between fantasy and reality. It's a different genre from fantasy because magical realism uses a substantial amount of realistic detail and employs magical elements to make a point about reality, while fantasy stories are set in a different reality. In magical realism the magical elements are extended metaphors—words and imagery used as representative or symbolic of something else—that often are symbolic of a character's emotions and inner world.

Coming of Age

Coming-of-age stories focus on the growth of a protagonist (typically a teenager) from childhood to adulthood. Though coming-of-age stories often also fit into other genres with all the action, adventure, mystery, suspense and romance that might entail, they can emphasise dialogue or internal monologue over action. The plot points are usually emotional changes within the characters. Many young-adult fantasy novels have a strong coming-of-age element.

Women's Fiction

Women's fiction is an umbrella term for women-centred books that focus on women's life experiences and are marketed to female readers. Women's fiction often has a romantic element but is not a romance as such, because it has other elements layered in, and the plot is driven by the main character's emotional journey towards a more fulfilled self, not her romance with another person.

And Many More Subgenres

Being specific and niching down your book helps you to sell it, and there are many subgenres within the above categories. For instance, steampunk, a subgenre of speculative fiction, features a late nineteenth century or early twentieth century setting but with steam-powered and clockwork inventions and machines.

Under thrillers and suspense, we have crime thrillers, domestic thrillers, financial thrillers, historical thrillers, legal thrillers, medical thrillers, military thrillers and so on.

Under science fiction, we have alien invasion, alternate history, colonisation science fiction, cyberpunk, first contact, galactic empire, genetic engineering, post-apocalyptic, space opera, time travel and so on.

Some mystery subgenres are amateur sleuths, cosy mysteries, hard-boiled mysteries, police procedurals, women sleuths, traditional detectives and so on.

In the fantasy genre, we can have dark fantasy, action and adventure, epic, humorous, sword and sorcery, military, myths and legends, superhero, historical and so on.

When Inspiration Hits

When inspiration for writing a novel hits in a powerful way, the decision on whether or not to write your story is taken care of. Inspiration blows all concerns out the door, and you find yourself writing anyway, simply because you just have to get the story down. You find yourself immersed in the world of your characters, and the story reveals itself as you type. It's an exciting time.

After you've had a seed of an idea sitting at the back of your mind for a while, anything might set off the level of inspiration needed for you to start typing: music, a photo, someone walking down the street, a conversation you overhear, a sunset, a dream, a movie or TV show, or a book or short story. For me it was a book. I found a book with the dramatic atmosphere and writing style I wanted in my book. I hadn't known how I wanted to approach my subject matter until I read it, and when I finished the book, it was as if a plug had been removed, and the words began to flow.

Images of scenes from the story appeared in my mind at all sorts of strange times. I remember stopping the car and making notes because a scene from *Lethal Inheritance* was burning in my brain, demanding to be released into the world. I discovered that if I wrote when the scene first appeared, my writing was easier and more immediate, more atmospheric, so I tended to stop what I was doing and go and write. Three in the morning was often a time of inspiration, and I'd write for a couple of hours, then go back to bed for a couple more hours of sleep before I had to get up and go to work. I lost a lot of sleep, but the thrill of uncovering a story more than made up for it.

Before that, I'd deliberated over whether to write the book or not, but once the inspiration started flowing, the power of it was so insistent that I felt I had no choice but to write. It was as if the story existed somewhere, and I just had to reveal it to the world.

At the beginning of your novel-writing journey, write whatever comes to you. It might be little snippets—descriptions, conversations or scenes— or maybe you write the beginning of your story; it doesn't matter. At this stage, just let the words flow.

At some point, however, you need to pause your writing and consider some important points, otherwise you might write a lot of words that you have to discard later because they're going off on tangents all over the place or focusing on something that doesn't really contribute to the story. That's what I did. I discarded a lot of the first draft of my first book because I wasn't clear on the central plot points. All I had was a vague idea, and once I'd refined the concept, I found that a lot of what I'd written simply didn't fit. I'd written background more than story, but it's the story that's important. The time wasn't entirely wasted, however, as it was all good writing practise, but I would have saved myself time if I'd asked myself the following:

- Is the plot clear? Do I have a protagonist with an aim and an antagonist with a conflicting aim?
- What genre is it?
- What are my central themes?
- Who is my ideal reader?

PART TWO:
GETTING STARTED

*'Try any goddamn thing you like,
no matter how boringly normal or
outrageous. If it works, fine. If it
doesn't, toss it.'*
—Stephen King.

How To Set Up Your Word Document

Though there are various different programs that authors can use to write their books, editors generally still work in Word, so at some point, you'll need to put your book into a Word document. When working in Word, it's important to set your manuscript up properly right at the start to make navigating a long document easy and to save time and money when you get to editing. If you're self-publishing, it will make formatting easier as well.

Setting your document up in the right format from the beginning is much easier than trying to change things after you've written a draft. And if you leave it for your editor to do, you'll be paying them to do something that you could have done yourself. I have seen a manuscript that was supposedly edited, but the editor had done no formatting. This surprised me because navigating a manuscript without proper formatting, at least for chapter headings, is very difficult, which is why professional editors do basic formatting as part of the editing process. If authors set up their document with basic formatting from the start, then they not only save money at the editing stage but also navigating their manuscript is easy.

Many beginning writers make a separate file for each chapter because they don't know how to set up Word for easy navigating of long documents, but it's important for editors and publishers that you present the entire manuscript in a single file. Keep it and all the related content—such as character descriptions, worldbuilding notes and so on—in one folder on your computer. When making revisions, you can copy and paste the content that's about to be cut or changed and save it in a separate file named something like 'Scraps' for future reference if needed. And whenever you do a major rewrite or another draft, 'Save As' with a new filename so you don't lose your earlier work. You never know when you might want to retrieve something.

But how do you navigate around a 90,000-word book? This is where correct set-up is so important, and the navigation pane is your key.

Navigation Pane

Go to the View menu and check Navigation Pane (under Ruler). This tool allows you to navigate around your book quickly and efficiently, and it has a search bar at the top. If you click the little arrow on the right of the search bar, you also get access to the find-and-replace function and other options.

To have your chapter headings show up in this navigation pane, use Word's built-in styles—Heading 1, Heading 2, Heading 3 and so on. You can either select them on the Home menu/ribbon, or right-click on what you've written, select Styles, click the little arrow, and choose the style you want.

Chapter Headings

I know you want to make your manuscript look like the finished product with pretty headings, but—unless you know how to modify the inbuilt styles and do it that way—it's better that you don't. If you don't work within Word's styles framework, the headings will not show up in the navigation pane, making them useless for helping you navigate a long document. If you want to change them, you'll have to go through and change them all individually.

Just use Word's inbuilt headings, and don't worry about how they look while you're writing. Once all your headings are set as a style, you can modify the style (as explained below) and change all the headings of that style at once.

On Word's Home menu/ribbon, you'll find the standard headings—Heading 1, 2, 3 and so on. Use these and they'll show up in the navigation pane. This allows you to easily go to a particular chapter— just click on it in the navigation pane—and you'll be able to rearrange parts of your manuscript by dragging the section headings around.

The standard headings appear in blue and are left justified. You can change their formatting, but keeping it simple is better for editors and publishers.

How to Modify a Style

To modify a style, right-click on what you've written, select Styles, right-click the style you wish to modify and choose Modify.

In the Modify dialogue box, you can easily centre the heading and change the font and its size.

And if you want to set some space before or after the heading, go to the bottom left and click on Format, then choose Paragraph, and you'll see a section called Spacing. Use this section to set how many lines you want blank before and after the heading. While you're there, if you want the heading centred, go to Indentation and choose None under Special. Do not choose First Line.

If you want a page break before the heading, go to Line and Page Breaks in the Paragraph menu and select Page Break Before.

The Normal Style

The best normal style for the publishing industry is black Times New Roman, 12-point with 1.5- or 2-line spacing. Times New Roman is a universal font across computers, so everyone will be able to read it. It is also a serif font, which makes it easier on your eyes—and your editor's eyes—than a non-serif font. You can write in whatever font you want, but when submitting it to industry professionals of any kind, make sure it's this industry standard. Fancy fonts make you look like an amateur who hasn't done your research.

To alter the normal style, right-click on some normal text, select Styles, right-click on Normal style and choose Modify. Choose the font (Times New Roman) and size (12pt) in black.

Click the drop-down arrow under Format at the bottom left of the dialogue box, choose

Paragraph, and in the Spacing section, set the line spacing to 1.5 or 2. In the Indentation area there under Special, click First line. This stops you from manually indenting each paragraph. Instead, when you hit Enter on your computer, the next line will automatically have an indent. Manual indents are a formatting nightmare. If you use them, then later on, you or someone else will have to go through and remove them all.

When modifying a heading style to centre it, don't set First line indent, but when setting up the normal style for fiction writing, do set the indentation to First line.

No-Indent Style

You can also set up a no-indent style for use at the beginning of chapters and sections. Correct book formatting has no indents for new sections after headings and scene breaks, so doing this will make your manuscript look more professional. If you plan to format the book yourself, then it's important to do this. Follow the process above to get into the Modify dialogue box, then name the new style, and in the Indentation area of the Paragraph dialogue box, make sure that First line is unchecked.

Set up the Quick Access Toolbar

You can customise the Quick Access Toolbar at the top of Word by adding the menu items you use regularly. This makes finding them much quicker and easier.

In any menu, right-click on the tool you want to add and click Add to Quick Access Toolbar. Click Customise the Ribbon to change the order of the tools.

Here's what I have on my quick access toolbar:

- Save
- Undo/Redo
- Navigation Pane
- Bookmark
- Comment
- Page Break
- Track Changes
- Word Count
- Thesaurus
- Change Case
- Bullet Points
- Decrease Indent
- Increase Indent
- Link

Comments and Bookmarks

Bookmarks are another handy way of navigating your document. They make it easy to find parts you think you'll want to go back to. Your editor might use these as well as comments, so you'll need to familiarise yourself with how they work.

Bookmarks

- Click your cursor where you want the bookmark to be.
- Go to the Insert menu and find Bookmarks in the Links section. Click on Bookmarks, and in the dialogue box that comes up, write a name for the bookmark with no spaces.
- Click on the Add button.
- To go to a bookmark already made, open the Bookmark dialogue box as above, select the bookmark you want to navigate to and click Go To.
- I find it convenient to have the Bookmark icon on my Quick Access Toolbar—right-click on it in the Insert menu and select Add to Quick Access Toolbar.

Comments

You'll need to know how to read comments made by anyone reviewing your manuscript. Go to the Review menu and click Show Comments. The Previous and Next buttons will take you to the previous or the next comment to save you having to scroll through the document to find them. The arrow in the Show Comments box allows you to choose Contextual or List to display them. List is useful if you want to see all the comments in a list rather than where they appear in the manuscript.

The Template

Now you're ready to start writing. Choose a blank template and work on that. Don't worry about setting a book size. Editors and publishers want the manuscript in whatever your default blank template is—A4 or Letter depending on your country.

How to Begin Writing – A Quick Start Guide

You've decided to write your novel, but how do you begin? Of course, you could just write and see what happens, and that's always fine, but if you consider a few things first, you can save yourself time and headaches. This chapter introduces you to elements that I will go into more deeply in later chapters.

An Introduction to Point of View

Can your story be told all from the perspective of one person? If so, consider writing it in first-person POV. Use 'I' did this, and 'I' did that, and so on when referring to the POV character. When you write in first person, you can't include anything seen from the perspective of another character.

The central character can only know what another person might be thinking from observing, and describing for the reader their facial expressions, tone of voice and gestures.

If you need more than one character's perspective to tell the story, then use third-person POV. Third person uses the pronouns 'he', 'she' and 'they' as in, *He ate the ice cream*. There are two kinds of third-person points of view.

Omniscient point of view is written from the perspective of an all-knowing narrator. They know what everyone is thinking and feeling and what is hiding around the corner. The important thing to understand when writing in omniscient POV is that there should be only one voice, that of the narrator, and even though they can see the thoughts of every character, it is advisable not to include many different characters' thought processes in one scene because it quickly becomes confusing for the reader. I suggest that beginning writers avoid this point of view. It's too remote for many modern readers, less immediate than the alternatives and hard to do well.

Third-person-intimate point of view is written from the perspective of a character and in that character's voice but using the pronoun 'he' or 'she' to refer to him or her. The language used is what that POV character would use if they were telling the story, so the reader sees the action through the POV character's eyes. This is used when an author wants to show more than one perspective but wants the reader to identify more deeply with a character than is possible in omniscient. For this reason, it usually involves changing from one intimate point of view to another, and this is where the writing can fall into head hopping.

Head hopping refers to abrupt changes in point of view such that the reader doesn't know whose head they're in, or they're being knocked from one character's thoughts and feelings to another like a ball in a tennis game. This can be very confusing for readers and so is something to be avoided. It also indicates that the writer hasn't done sufficient research on writing craft. Refer to my book *The Elements of Active Prose: Writing Tips to Make Your Prose Shine* for details on how to avoid head hopping.

If you have only a couple of character's perspectives, you can have alternating chapters with one first-person POV in one chapter and another first-person POV in the next chapter, but it's best not to use that for more than a couple of characters, and some people don't like even that. First-person POV is best used with just one main character, your protagonist.

It's advisable not to have too many points of view. The fewer points of view, the more you create an intimate feeling in the story. Five is generally agreed to be the maximum, and five is a lot.

Basic Plot

You don't need to have your story all plotted out, but you should have the main plot elements decided on—know your protagonist (central character), protagonist's aims, antagonist (the bad guy or disruptive element), antagonist's aims, and how they clash to create the dramatic tension. I also suggest at a minimum that you have a beginning, a middle and an end in mind. If you don't start with something tangible in the plot department, then when you or a beta reader looks back over it, you may discover that, at best, it doesn't hang together, and at worst, it doesn't actually have a story. You're then faced with a complete rethink that usually leads to throwing a lot out, rewriting large parts of it and writing new material. You can always change or develop your rudimentary plot further as you write.

Even if you like to write from the seat of your pants and not be stuck to an outline, it's still important to have a basic plot in mind.

Are You a Plotter or a Pantser?

Pantsing (also known as winging it) is the term authors use to refer to writing without a fixed outline. An author who adopts the pantsing approach to writing is called a pantser. A plotter is someone who has an outline that they follow. It doesn't matter what approach you take, but it's good to consider what will work best for you before or soon after you begin writing.

I suspect that many authors, like me, fall between these two extremes in that they have a plotline and some degree of structure in mind or written out, but they don't force themselves to stick to that outline as they write. That way they get the benefit of allowing their imagination to throw in unexpected twists as they write, while avoiding the possibility that they may wander so much that they end up with something with no shape.

I think it's a good idea for beginning writers to have some kind of outline, but to be flexible enough with it to change if needed or if they become inspired to take another direction. Certainly, you need a plotline, because without that, you don't really have a story.

I plotted my first books out in detail. Later books, after I became an experienced author, I wrote without plotting for the first half of the book, then I sat down and plotted out the rest.

Whatever approach you plan to take, my advice is to be flexible.

Characters

Who are they? What are their likes and dislikes, and strengths and weaknesses—make sure they have some weaknesses, because perfect characters are boring. What quirks/mannerisms/habits—speech or physical—do they have? How are they different from each other? What do they look like, speak like, think about the issues in your book?

Some people write these kinds of things down before they start, while others just have the ideas in their minds and allow the details to come out as they write. Either is fine, so long as you have considered the questions above. You don't have to have all the details decided when you start, but if you don't have a picture of your characters in your mind, it's a good idea to write down their descriptions to help with continuity.

In my first book, I had to keep looking back to my last description to see what colour eyes or hair I'd given them. I soon discovered that it was wise to keep such details in a separate file called 'Characters'.

Where to Start

You don't need to begin at the beginning of your story. If authors did that, every story would begin with the birth of the protagonist, and that would be very dull. The beginning of a book needs to grab the reader, hold on to them and not let go, so choose an exciting part of the story to dive into. You'd be surprised at how often, as an editor, I suggest cutting some of the first part of a manuscript and beginning the story at a later stage.

Avoid prologues as well. It's better to throw readers directly into the story. But if you must have one, keep it short and snappy, and stick to the essential points.

Information and Worldbuilding

Fantasy and science fiction books need information to help readers make sense of magical or technical systems, and different worlds and cultures, and other books might need historical facts, personal histories and other relevant backstory. The question we need to ask is how much information to put in, so that what isn't needed can be left out.

The tendency for some authors is to include too much information, while others have the opposite problem and tend not to include enough. It's easier to add information in, however, than to delete it, so I recommend putting in less than you think you need. Readers do not need to know everything we know about our story. They are quite capable of putting suggestions together to form a picture.

Revising my early writing efforts included a process of paring back the details I'd included in my first draft until I had just enough but no more than was necessary.

Whatever you think you need to include, make sure it's as succinct as possible, pepper it throughout the action, and don't let it slow the story down. I suggest that you jot down a few points on what you really must include, just so you aren't tempted to put in swathes of unnecessary information or leave out something important. Then ask yourself if you can show that material through events or by how people act or interact in a scene. That's a much better way to get the details across than just telling the reader about it.

Now You're Ready to Start

After you've considered these points, just sit down and write, and stick at it until that first draft is completed.

Plot and Structure

It's essential that authors understand the basic plot elements that create a solid foundation for a story.

The Protagonist

The protagonist is the main point-of-view character in your story. They are the person the reader follows and in whom they become emotionally invested. While you may have multiple characters and several whose point of view you share, it's best to have one primary protagonist and introduce them early so the reader knows who the story is about.

The Goal

What is the protagonist's aim in the story? What must they achieve, solve, fix or discover? This goal should be clear to the reader by around the 15% mark of your novel. If you leave it later than 25% into the story, you risk losing readers. The goal tells the reader what the story is about.

The Antagonist

Who or what is preventing the protagonist from achieving their goal? The antagonist is a vital element of your story, as they create tension and conflict. While your antagonist can be a non-human disruptive element, such as a psychological issue or physical terrain, having a person involved often leads to a stronger story due to the unpredictability of human behaviour.

Different Plot Structures

It's helpful to familiarise yourself with various classic plot structures. These can serve as a guide when creating your own unique story.

Three-Act Structure

The three-act structure is a classic storytelling framework that divides the plot into three parts: the setup, the confrontation, and the resolution.

- **Setup**: Introduce the protagonist, setting and their goal. (First 25%.)
- **Confrontation**: The protagonist faces obstacles and conflicts leading to a turning point. (Middle 50%.)
- **Resolution**: The climax of the story, where the protagonist either achieves their goal or fails, followed by the denouement, which is the final resolution or tying up of loose ends. (Last 25%.)

Plot Point Placement for a Three-Act Structure

Hook (Start of Act One)

The hook comes within the first few pages of your story. It could be the opening line, but it doesn't have to be. Your hook is something that makes the reader want to read on. Something that raises a question or intrigues them. I look into how to hook readers in more detail in the 'How to Write a Good

Beginning Paragraph' chapter later in this book.

Inciting Incident (Middle of Act One)

Early in the story, something needs to happen to set the story in motion. This usually happens in the first half of Act One, at around 10%–15% of the way through the story. I write more about this in a later chapter.

First Plot Point (Start of Act Two, 25%)

The first plot point comes at around 25% through the story. This is where everything changes. You've set up the character and their world, given the character impetus to take a step into something new, and now a big change propels the story forward. Your protagonist will spend the next quarter of the book reacting to this change and its implications.

Second Plot Point (Middle of Act Two, 50%)

At the midpoint of your novel, something major happens that jolts your character into action. Up until now they have been reacting to the inciting incident and first plot point, but this is a major turning point, after which they'll be actively fighting for some goal they're determined to pursue. For the rest of Act Two, you keep raising the stakes, adding more challenges for your protagonist to overcome.

Third Plot Point (End of Act Two, 75%)

The third plot point normally marks a major setback in your protagonist's attempt to achieve their goal. It's their lowest point, their darkest hour, perhaps a failure of some kind. The stakes are high, and things haven't gone their way, no matter how hard they've tried, and they might feel tempted to give up. But after this plot point, they regain their energy and become determined to reach their goal. This leads into the climax of your novel.

Climax (Middle of Act Three)

After the tension building through the beginning of Act Three, we come to the climax of the story where the protagonist faces the antagonist (or antagonistic force). Usually, the protagonist wins, but it's a struggle and may require some kind of sacrifice. The whole story leads up to this moment, so it needs to be engaging and satisfying.

Resolution (Second Half of Act Three)

After the climax, where the protagonist strikes the final blow against the villain, the rest of Act Three is the resolution (or denouement) that shows the new reality and its implications for the protagonist and the world. Loose ends are tied up and hints left of the possibility of further adventures.

Hero's Journey

The Hero's Journey is a narrative template that involves a hero embarking on an adventure, facing and overcoming trials, and returning transformed. Popularised by Joseph Campbell, this structure can be found in many novels, movies and myths.

- **Ordinary world**: Introduce the protagonist and their normal life.
- **Call to adventure**: The protagonist receives a challenge or invitation to embark on a journey.
- **Refusal of the call**: The protagonist initially resists or hesitates to accept the challenge.
- **Meeting the mentor**: The protagonist encounters a wise figure who provides guidance and support.
- **Crossing the threshold**: The protagonist commits to the journey and enters a new world.
- **Tests, allies and enemies**: The protagonist faces challenges, makes friends and encounters foes.
- **Approach to the inmost cave**: The protagonist prepares for a significant ordeal.
- **Ordeal**: The protagonist confronts their greatest fear or challenge.
- **Reward**: The protagonist achieves their goal or receives something valuable.
- **The road back**: the protagonist starts their journey back to the ordinary world.
- **Resurrection**: the protagonist faces a final test or battle, resulting in personal transformation.
- **Return with the elixir**: the protagonist returns home, sharing their newfound wisdom or treasure with others.

Seven-Point Story Structure

The seven-point story structure is a flexible framework that can help you create a well-paced and engaging plot.

- **Hook**: An opening scene that grabs the reader's attention and introduces the protagonist.
- **First plot point**: A major event that sets the protagonist on their path and introduces the antagonist.
- **First pinch point**: The antagonist applies pressure, forcing the protagonist to react.
- **Midpoint**: A turning point where the protagonist begins to take control and actively pursue their goal.
- **Second pinch point**: The antagonist applies even more pressure, raising the stakes.
- **Second plot point**: The final piece of information or event that propels the story towards its climax.
- **Resolution**: The climax and resolution of the story, where the protagonist either achieves their goal or fails.

You can choose a structure that works best for your novel and adapt it to suit your story. The minimum structure for a successful story is:

1. The setup;
2. The confrontation;
3. The resolution.

Outlining Your Novel

Outlining your novel provides a structured approach to developing your story, ensuring that you have a clear roadmap to follow from start to finish. Whether you're a plotter or a pantser, a simple outline can help you stay on track and maintain consistency throughout your narrative. What follows are the steps you can take to create an effective outline for your novel, but it's only a suggestion. Your outline can be as brief or detailed as you wish—whatever comes naturally to you. I start my novels with only a brief outline and then return to it and make it more detailed as I write, once more of the story reveals itself to me.

1. Brainstorm Ideas

Begin your outlining process by brainstorming all the ideas you have for your story. This includes thinking about your characters, settings, potential conflicts and any themes you want to explore. Don't worry about organising these ideas just yet—this step is about letting your creativity flow freely. You might consider using mind maps, lists or even sketches to capture your thoughts.

2. Organise Your Ideas

Once you have a wealth of ideas, start organising them into related categories. This could involve grouping elements related to character development, worldbuilding and plot points. For example, you might separate notes on your protagonist's backstory from details about the world's geography. This organisation helps you see the big picture and identify connections between different elements of your story.

3. Choose a Plot Structure

Selecting a plot structure that resonates with your story is a crucial step in outlining. Your chosen structure will serve as a framework for your outline, guiding the pacing and progression of your narrative. For instance, if you're using the three-act structure, you'll plan out the setup, confrontation, and resolution. You don't need to follow an established structure, of course, but studying them so you become familiar with their elements and concepts—such as plot points and stakes—will help you create an engaging structure for your book.

4. Develop Your Characters

A compelling story requires well-developed characters. Begin fleshing out your protagonist, antagonist and supporting characters by exploring their motivations, backgrounds and character arcs. Consider their strengths, weaknesses, and how they will evolve over the course of the story. This development will not only help you write more authentic characters but also ensure that their actions drive the plot forward.

5. Establish the Setting

A vivid setting can enhance your story and make it more immersive. Define the key elements of your world, such as geography, history, culture and technology. Whether you're writing a contemporary novel or a high-fantasy epic, consider how these elements will influence the story and the characters. For example, a dystopian setting will shape the characters' outlooks and decisions in significant ways.

6. Identify Key Plot Points

Determine the major events and turning points in your story. These are the moments that will shape your narrative and keep readers engaged. Align these plot points with your chosen structure to ensure a cohesive and compelling story arc. Key plot points might include the inciting incident, the midpoint twist, the climax and the resolution. Each should move the story forward and challenge your characters in meaningful ways.

7. Create a Scene-by-Scene Outline

Finally, break your story down into individual scenes. For each scene, detail what happens, which characters are involved, and how it contributes to the overall plot. This scene-by-scene outline serves as a detailed roadmap, helping you maintain narrative flow and pacing. Remember, your outline is a flexible tool—it's okay to make changes as you write and discover new directions for your story.

Worldbuilding

The word 'worldbuilding' refers to the creation of a fictional world. When writing fiction, especially fantasy and science fiction (speculative fiction), you have the freedom to create your own rules, cultures and geography. Worldbuilding is essential because it helps your readers to understand and relate to your characters and the environments in which they exist.

Worldbuilding is not just about creating a setting for your story; it's about creating a complete world that is rich in detail, history and culture. It's about creating a world that feels real, even if it doesn't exist anywhere except in your imagination. Worldbuilding is an essential part of any speculative fiction writing process.

Types of Fictional Worlds

There are several types of fictional worlds, including fantasy, sci-fi, dystopian and more. Fantasy worlds are filled with magic and mythical creatures, while sci-fi worlds are often set in the future and may include advanced technology. Dystopian worlds are usually bleak and oppressive, while post-apocalyptic worlds are set after a significant event that has changed the world.

Whatever type of world you choose to build, it's important to remember that your world needs to be consistent and believable. Every detail needs to be thought out, from the geography to the culture and history. Though you don't need to tell the reader all the things you know about the world, you do need to know them yourself.

Elements of Worldbuilding

To create a believable fictional world, you need to include several elements.

Geography

The geography of your world will influence the cultures and societies that exist within it. Think about the climate, the terrain and the natural resources that your world has to offer.

Culture

The culture of your world will be influenced by the geography, history and the people who live there. Think about the customs, traditions and beliefs of the people in your world.

History

The history of your world will shape the current state of your world. Think about the significant events that have occurred in your world and how they have impacted the people who live there.

Magic System

If your world includes magic, you need to think about how it works. Consider the rules and limitations of magic in your world.

A Step-by-Step Worldbuilding Guide

- To create a captivating world, start by identifying the aspect that excites you the most.
- Jot down the rules and regulations that govern the inhabitants of your world. This includes their political system, who's in charge, and whether magic exists, among other things. Setting restrictions will make your world more believable and functional.
- Determine the type of world you want to create, such as a dystopian or fantasy world, and establish the tone and mood accordingly.
- Describe the environment in detail, including weather patterns, natural resources and how people interact with the land. When developing a fictional world, it's important to consider the environment and its impact on the inhabitants.
- Define the culture of the world, including beliefs, religion, sacred customs and celebrations. Creating rich and meaningful characters is key to bringing the world to life. Additionally, determining the language used by the inhabitants, including any taboo words or phrases, can provide a source of conflict.
- Identify the world's history. When creating

a fictional world, it's important to give it a comprehensive backstory that includes information about conflicts, such as wars, enemies, rival races and antagonists. You don't have to lay out all this information for the reader, but the author needs to know it for themselves so that they write a story that reflects that history. Having a history for your world adds depth to it and makes it more relatable.

- To get inspiration, you can review how other writers have answered similar worldbuilding questions in their own novels.

Mapping Your Fictional World

Mapping your fictional world is an important part of the worldbuilding process for imaginary worlds, and fantasy books often include a map. Mapping helps you visualise the world and keep track of the various locations and landmarks within it.

There are several tools and techniques that you can use to map your world, including online map-making tools, drawing software or even pen and paper. Whatever method you choose, make sure that your map is consistent with the geography and culture of your world.

Developing Characters Within Your Fictional World

When developing characters within your fictional world, it's important to consider the cultural influences and backstory of your characters. The culture of your fictional world will influence the beliefs and values of your characters, while their backstory will shape their personalities and motivations.

Consider the different cultures and societies within your world and how they might influence your characters. Think about the history of your world and how it might impact your characters' experiences and beliefs.

Incorporating Worldbuilding into Your Plot and Story Arc

Worldbuilding should be an integral part of your plot and story arc. Your world should influence the events that occur in your story, and the events in your story should shape the world that you have created.

When incorporating worldbuilding into your plot and story arc, make sure that it's done in a way that feels natural and organic. Avoid info-dumping or overwhelming your readers with too much information at once.

Common Worldbuilding Mistakes to Avoid

There are several common worldbuilding mistakes to avoid, including inconsistencies, lack of details, and overwhelming your readers with too much information. When building your fictional world, make sure that every detail is consistent and believable. Avoid leaving out important details, but don't overwhelm your readers with too much information at once.

Writing Characters Readers Care About

Writing characters that readers care about is a vital skill for any author who wants to write well. In novel writing, story is king, because without a great story—a strong plot with dramatic tension to glue the reader to the page—a reader will lose interest, but without characters that readers care about, the novel will fall flat. If a reader doesn't care about a character, then even if you put them in life-threatening situations, the dramatic tension doesn't take hold of the reader, and the story loses its power.

I have read books where I've said to myself, 'Why should I care what happens to you?' I don't finish such books; why would I? Reading a book is a big time commitment, and readers don't want to spend a lot of time with characters they don't care about.

The characters we care most easily about are the ones we like, so it's good to make your central character(s) likeable, but that doesn't mean they should have no faults. Perfection is boring, and readers quickly lose interest. You might want your protagonist to be a hero, but hero or heroine is not a character description; it's merely a description of one kind of behaviour that a character may exhibit. Our hero or heroine might save the day, but they must be much more than a saviour if readers are to relate to them and care about them.

What Readers Want in a Character

Readers want characters they can relate to, and that means characters who seem like real people, who have the kinds of issues and challenges real people have. We relate to those who are like ourselves in some respect, and one thing that all human beings share is that we all have personal challenges. Anyone who thinks they are without fault has the fault of lack of awareness of their own faults.

Even if your protagonist is a robot or an alien, they need to have human characteristics if you want your readers to relate to them. A secondary character or antagonist in a speculative fiction book could be so alien that they don't appear to have human characteristics, but they still need to have clear reasons for behaving as they do. They need a perspective on their world and the events of the story that makes them behave as they do and react as they do.

Protagonists Readers Hate

Readers don't want to like all the characters in a book. We love to hate the bad guys and those around the central character (protagonist) who cause them frustration, so some of your secondary characters can be unpleasant or annoying people, and your antagonists should be someone readers can hate for at least one reason. But don't make your central character, the protagonist, unlikeable, because they're the one you want readers to be rooting for.

When I choose books to read, I read reader reviews, and it's clear to me that, in general, readers dislike protagonists who:

- are whiny
- are shallow—concerned only with surface appearances, or overly concerned with relatively unimportant things, like their clothes

and makeup

- are perfect—perfect characters are boring and unbelievable
- require rescuing all the time—central characters should grow as the story progresses
- are one dimensional—for instance, only evil with no redeeming features or understandable motivations
- are cold-hearted and care only about themselves
- consistently make stupid mistakes—like getting into a car with a stranger
- the narrator says the character is something, but they don't behave like it—like a university graduate who does things that show a lack of intelligence

Characters Readers Love

Your protagonist should be someone who readers relate to easily, someone believable with real human characteristics and challenges, and preferably someone readers will come to love, or, at least, like and care about. When readers like a character, they get very enthusiastic about the book they appear in, and they'll read every book you write about that character.

Don't make all your characters likeable, of

course, just the main one. Readers love characters who:

- are decent or trying to be
- are naturally funny, but not flippant or forced
- care about people other than themselves
- have endearing characteristics, like wayward hair that drives them crazy
- have the kinds of challenges readers are familiar with, such as lack of self-confidence or having trouble trusting people
- are honest about their issues and are working on them
- grow as the story progresses
- are 'noble'

Noble Characters

Noble characters are the heroic kind, and everyone loves a hero. Our most beloved stories are populated with noble characters. Even if they don't save the day or save anyone, even if they are physically weak or without any special skills, they have noble characteristics that inspire readers. They are, to some extent, role models of the best kind of human being. They have the following kinds of characteristics:

- They care about people, both individuals

and groups.

- Ethics are important to them both personally and socially.
- They have a strong sense of what's right and wrong and always try to do what's right.
- They are wise or have some insight into situations or are trying to make wise decisions.
- They are aware of their faults and weaknesses, or trying to be, and though they fall prey to them sometimes, they work to overcome them.
- They fight for what is right with unflagging determination.
- They'll protect the weak and fight on behalf of those who can't fight for themselves.
- They don't give up when the going gets tough. They may want to give up; they may even give up for a short period of time, but they will always pick themselves up and get back to work fighting whatever evil they're facing.

Noble characters are not perfect; note the words 'try to' and 'trying to' in this list and the points on being aware of their faults and weaknesses. What makes a character noble is that they have noble motivations. Essentially, they're someone with some degree of wisdom and compassion or someone trying to act with wisdom and compassion.

Writing Characters

Three methods come to mind when thinking about how to write characters. One method is not better than another, and an author may use one method for some characters and another for others, or one method may come more naturally to an author than another.

They Appear in Your Mind

In this case, the author simply knows the characters at one glance. They come into the author's mind along with the story as part of the creative process. The author sees them and gets to know them as they write. It's as if the author doesn't create the character, but rather that the character exists somewhere in their imagination, and the author uncovers the character as the story reveals itself to them.

This is how my characters come to me, and the idea that the characters exist in a world I link to in my imagination is a concept that I go into in my novel *Worlds Within Worlds*.

You Create Them

Here the author consciously creates the characters, often with the help of a character-description form of some kind. The author comes up with a name and gender, and then lists details such as age, appearance, where they live, their occupation, their childhood background, family information, education, relationships, strengths, weaknesses, personal issues, what is important to them, what they care about, what they think about the issues explored in the novel and so on.

They Appear and You Refine Them

This is basically a combination of the other two methods. In this case, the author gets a sense of who the character is and starts writing, but at some point, they realise that they need to know more about the character or they're having continuity errors, so they set up a character-description document, write down what they know about the character and fill in the gaps.

I often do this for secondary characters, who simply haven't appeared as fully in my mind as the protagonist usually does. I also find it difficult to remember all aspects of different characters, so it's handy to have them written down somewhere where you can refer back to the details. This is important so that George doesn't start off with blue eyes and end up with green ones!

If a beta reader or your editor says that your characters need more development, then I recommend using a character-description form. You can download these from various sites on the web.

Using a Character-Description Form

The trick with using a character-description form is to use it to help your imagination seek the details of your character. So don't feel you have to fill in every part of the form; just fill in the main parts—name, gender, age, appearance, home, occupation, childhood and family background, education, relationships, strengths, weaknesses, personal issues, what is important to them—and then use the other parts of the form to get you thinking further. If something comes to mind, great; if not, just move on. The act of thinking about it is sufficient to set the process of deepening your character moving.

Character Development Tips

Once you know your character, you then must make sure that they act and react as such a character would. The easiest way to do that is to become the character as you write them. Never forget who you are as you write from that character's point of view. And, of course, you have to speak as they would speak, using the language such a character would use. If English is your character's second language, they'll not be speaking perfect English, and if they went to a posh school, they're unlikely to swear all the time.

Great authors are actors as well as writers; they play all the roles of all the characters in their work. Certainly, when I write, I write as if I am the character. In fact, I immerse myself so totally in that character and in that situation that I *am* the character. This was the one thing that I could do right from the start in my writing journey, and it's a good skill to develop if you want your characters to leap off the page.

Essential Points for Crafting Compelling Characters

- **Give them a backstory:** Develop a history for each character. Explore their past experiences, family dynamics, and the events that shaped their beliefs and desires.
- **Create clear motivations:** Understand what drives your characters, such as a desire for love, power, revenge, personal growth and so on.
- **Give them flaws:** Give your characters flaws that make them human and create internal conflicts.
- **Develop character arcs:** Plan how your characters will grow and change throughout the story, ensuring their development is believable and satisfying.
- **Create meaningful relationships:** Develop the relationships between your characters. Explore how they influence and challenge each other.
- **Give them distinctive voices:** Ensure each character has a unique way of speaking, reflecting their personality, background and emotions.

How to Write a Good Beginning Paragraph

The opening paragraph of a novel is the first impression your reader will have of your book. It's your chance to hook them in and keep them engaged throughout the entire story. A great opening paragraph can set the tone for the entire book and leave a lasting impression on your reader.

Think of the opening paragraph as a handshake. You want to make a good first impression and establish trust with your reader. If you fail to capture their attention in the first few sentences, it's likely they will put the book down and move on to something else.

Answering the following questions will help you create a clear and concise opening paragraph: Who is the main character? What is their goal? What is the setting?

Understanding Your Genre and Audience

Before you start writing your opening paragraph, it's essential to understand your genre and audience. Different genres have different expectations for their opening paragraphs. For example, a thriller may start with a fast-paced action scene, while a romance novel may start with a character in a setting that indicates the time and place in which the story unfolds.

Your audience is also essential to consider. Are you writing for young adults or adults? What are their interests and preferences? Knowing your audience will help you tailor your opening paragraph to their expectations and keep them engaged throughout the book.

The Elements of a Great Opening Paragraph

A great opening paragraph should include several elements to capture your reader's attention. First, it should establish the setting and introduce the main character. This helps the reader picture the scene and connect with the character.

Next, it should introduce the conflict or

problem the main character will face throughout the book. This creates tension and intrigue, making the reader want to read on and find out what happens next.

Finally, a great opening paragraph should have a strong hook. This could be a cliffhanger, a surprising statement, or a thought-provoking question. The hook should make the reader want to keep reading and find out more about the story.

A short sentence to start followed by a longer sentence also works well. The first sentence is snappy, and the following sentence gives more information to lead the reader further into the story.

Writing, Editing and Revising the Opening Paragraph

Don't worry about making the opening paragraph perfect the first time around—it rarely is. The first draft is just a starting point. Focus on getting your ideas down on paper with the aim of creating a compelling opening paragraph that will hook your reader.

After you've written the first draft, you can revise and edit your first paragraph right away or at any time during the writing process. I return to my opening paragraph many times during writing, looking at it again with fresh eyes. It's a process of refining ideas and making the writing more concise and engaging.

When you come to revise, start by reading your opening paragraph and making notes of any areas that feel weak or unclear. Then revise those areas to make your writing stronger and more impactful. I revised the first paragraph of my first novel around twenty-seven times as I learned more about the craft of writing.

Once you've made your revisions, read the paragraph again and make any final edits. Pay attention to the flow of the writing, and ensure that each sentence contributes to the overall impact.

Examples of Great Opening Paragraphs

To help you understand what makes a great opening paragraph, here are some examples from well-known novels:

- *'Mother died today. Or maybe yesterday, I don't know. I had a telegram from the home: "Mother passed away. Funeral tomorrow. Yours sincerely."* *That doesn't mean anything. It may have been yesterday.'* - Albert Camus, *The Stranger.*
- *'It was a bright cold day in April, and the clocks*

were striking thirteen.' - George Orwell, *1984*.

- *'No live organism can continue for long to exist sanely under conditions of absolute reality; even larks and katydids are supposed, by some, to dream. Hill House, not sane, stood by itself against its hills, holding darkness within; it had stood so for eighty years and might stand for eighty more. Within, walls continued upright, bricks met neatly, floors were firm, and doors were sensibly shut; silence lay steadily against the wood and stone of Hill House, and whatever walked there, walked alone...'* - Shirley Jackson, *The Haunting of Hill House*.
- *'The man in black fled across the desert and the gunslinger followed.'* - Stephen King, *The Dark Tower Volume 1: The Gunslinger*.

Each of these opening paragraphs captures the reader's attention and sets the tone for the entire book.

Essential Tips for Writing

The best tip I can give for writing well is: As you write, delve deep into your imagination and truly experience your story as if you are living it yourself. Craftsmanship can be learned as you refine and rewrite, but if your writing doesn't emerge from a deep immersion in your story, it will be superficial, and superficial writing does not result in engaged readers. A great book is a book that draws the reader right into the scenes, characters and events, a book in which readers can immerse themselves, and for that to happen, you as the author must first immerse yourself in your story.

Live Your Story

When I first started out as an author, I had no idea how to actually write, how to use words to express myself, but I have always had a great imagination, and I was able to immerse myself in the world of *Diamond Peak*, my young-adult fantasy series, such that, although my writing had a long way to go before it reached a publishable standard, I wrote in a way that evoked the atmosphere of the story. Even in its raw form, the story had a rough kind of power. Why? Because I lived it as I wrote it. I placed myself in each scene. I saw what the characters saw, thought what they thought and felt their emotions deeply. I wasn't just acting the point-of-view character; I was them.

Though after my first draft I had to embark on a long journey of learning how to improve my prose, I did, at least, have the raw material to work with. And you can do that too.

Set Up a Conducive Environment

Think about where you're going to write and when. Choose whatever time suits you and set it aside as your writing time. Write every day, even if it's only a couple of paragraphs. If you leave it too long between visits to your world, you'll lose momentum. Preferably, find a place where you can shut the door and even place a sign on the doorknob saying, 'Do not disturb.'

Set up your writing space in a way that is conducive to your immersion in the story. Maybe you need a view of the garden, or a clear desk, or maybe you need a dagger beside you, or a crystal ball, or a noticeboard filled with images to stimulate your imagination. Maybe you need a good sound system. Set up whatever you need to help you immerse yourself in your story. Make your writing space inspiring.

Sensory Stimulus

Writing well is writing such that the reader can hear, see, smell, touch and even taste the character's world and experience. Of course, to write that way, you must first experience your story through all those senses yourself. Luckily, there are ways to help you.

Aural Stimulus

Silence works best for me, but other authors write to music, and certainly if you find it hard to get into the story—this often happens in the sections that are hardest to write—then music can really help. Some authors have playlists that they later share with their fans. If music stimulates your imagination, then spend some time making a playlist that relates to characters, scenes or settings. Simple sounds can also be helpful. If you're writing a scene in a storm, find a recording of a storm to listen to as you write.

Visual Stimulus

When writing about a journey high in the mountains around a glacial lake and into ice caves, I searched for images of the kind of landscape I envisaged. I placed these images on the noticeboard above my computer so I could look up at them, not just to help me describe that kind of terrain, but also to help me to imagine myself there.

Images of people can be used to help you with your characterisation. You can even make up characters based on a photo you find online, or you can use an AI art generator to help you envisage your characters and settings.

Videos are particularly helpful when you write actions that you haven't experienced yourself, things like fighting, racing a motorbike or galloping a horse.

Sensual Stimulus

If you've forgotten what it feels like to stand in the rain, turn on the hose and get someone to spray you! If you've forgotten what a café smells like, go to a café. Visit a rainforest if you have a scene set in a rainforest, and pay attention to the smell, the feel of the mulch under your feet and the sound of your footsteps. You probably can't go to the top of a mountain, but you can try to imagine the clean air, the silence and the cold.

How does a straight whisky feel when you down it in one gulp? Go have a shot!

Writing someone swimming? Do you remember what it's like to float in the ocean? Go have a swim.

When writing fight scenes, I used to get my family to help me. I'd call my daughter or husband into my office and ask them to act out the scene with me to help me envisage just where our body parts would go and what move might naturally follow another. I got a couple of bruises from this, but I also got a clear idea of what my character was actually doing, and what was realistic for him or her to do in a certain situation. This helped me write accurate fight scenes.

How Much to Write

Of course, if you immerse yourself completely in a scene such that you experience it with all your senses, you might write more details than you need to, so it's important to know that we don't have to describe every single part of an action. Never put in so much detail that you slow down the story. The reader likes to feel that they are in the story, but they also want your story to keep moving along.

As the author, you will always have more information than you'll need. So tell the reader enough to stimulate their imagination, but not so much that you're leaving nothing for them to imagine themselves. If there is no reason for the reader to use their imagination or not enough cues to inspire their imagination, then you've removed the interactive aspect and much of the pleasure of reading. As with much in the craft of writing, it's all about balance, but at the first-draft stage, don't worry about that too much. Balance can be refined at the revision stage; just feel your story from inside your characters, and when you write, don't get bogged down with details.

Enjoy

If you enjoy your writing, your readers likely will as well, but many books have unpleasant scenes that you probably won't enjoy being immersed in; in these cases, enjoy the drama and the excitement. If your heart is pounding with terror, you'll be more likely to write in a way that makes the reader's heart pound, and that's the mark of good writing.

Writing the First Draft

Writing the first draft of a book can be exciting or frustrating, and often it's both. Some authors love writing the first draft; others hate it. Why? Because it's wonderful to finally get your ideas down, but writing the first draft can tend to take over your life. When I write first drafts, inspiration rules me. I am its slave, and that can be difficult, especially for those who are competing with a book for your attention. But at the same time, immersing yourself totally in the world of your stories and characters is the way to get the best creative writing.

Forget Rules

At the first draft stage, no matter whether you are writing to an outline or just going where the story takes you as you write, you shouldn't concern yourself with technique. Forget grammar, punctuation and rules of any kind. Forget it all and just write. The first draft is about getting your creativity flowing and getting the story written; that's all.

Let your creativity soar!

The time to consider the fine points of craftspersonship is when you revise, rewrite and edit the story.

Immerse Yourself

If you immerse yourself in the world of your characters such that you hear what they hear, see what they see, smell what they smell, hear their thoughts, feel their feelings and know their hopes and fears, then you will write well. That's the challenge of the first draft. Get inside the characters and into their world so you can draw the reader in. Readers want an immersive experience, and you can't draw them in if you haven't been on the inside yourself. The idea is to write from your protagonist's point of view as if you are the character, even if you're writing in third person. In third-person-intimate point of view, the writing should be as if told in the words of the point-of-view character, and doing that is a lot easier if you *are* that character as you write.

Even as an editor, I immerse myself in the world of the book to make the best choices to reveal each story in the best possible way. I try to be each character, so my choices strengthen the character's voice, not diminish it.

If your characters are having a hard time, it can be painful to get inside their hearts and minds, but if you can do that, then you will be writing what you know, because you will have experienced it in your imagination.

If you find it hard to become your protagonist, at least see if you can watch their story unfold as if you're watching a movie in an immersive movie theatre with full surround sound.

As mentioned above, some authors find it helpful to listen to music or look at images when imagining scenes and writing descriptions.

Who's Writing This Story?

I always feel that I am not so much writing a story as uncovering it. It's not my story; it's my characters' story. I'm just transferring it to the page. I follow my characters' leads—they know their story better than I—and sometimes they take over the writing and lead me where I never thought the story would go.

So don't force your story into your outline if it doesn't want to go that way. An outline is just a guide, something that gives you overall direction; it should be flexible. There may be a better way to move the story forward that you hadn't thought of, a more interesting way. That happened to me in my third book, *Demon's Grip*. I felt scared to go in the new direction because I didn't know where it would lead, but I remembered Stephen King's advice (below) and kept digging deep to reveal a deeper version of the story. That willingness to step outside my outline took that book from ordinary to extraordinary, and it happened because a character said, 'Yes,' when I had planned for her to say, 'No.'

At first, I said, 'No, we're not going that way,' but she insisted that her way was the way the story happened. I actually had an argument with one of my characters!

'This is how it happened,' she told me. 'And it's my story, not yours. You're just telling it for me.'

I had to concede that she was right.

In his book, *On Writing*, Stephen King says, 'Stories are found things, like fossils in the ground ... Stories are relics, part of an undiscovered pre-existing world.' He says that writers should be like archaeologists, excavating for as much of the story as they can find.

Voice

One of the reasons for not concerning yourself with grammar and so forth at the first-draft stage is so your voice can come out. Your voice as an author is your perspective on the world and your style of writing, but your characters also have voices, and they may not speak in perfect grammar—how many people do? Each point-of-view character should have their own voice, their own way of seeing the world, and if you focus too much on writing 'correctly' at this stage, your characters can all end up sounding the same.

An author's voice is important. It's what makes readers come back for more of your books. They recognise a style and perspective that, if it appeals, they want more of. When a publisher looks at your book, a strong voice will grab them, whereas a voice that sounds like every other author's voice will sound uninteresting to them. As a publisher reading submissions, I know this personally. A strong voice can be the single reason I will request a full manuscript. So don't try to write like anyone else. Just write!

And do not use AI to write the prose for your book. That's a sure way to sound generic, and you will never find your unique voice if you have someone or something else do it for you.

Don't Try to Write Well

Trying to write well is a trap. I know because I fell into it with my first book. If you try too hard, your writing might come out formal and stilted, or overwritten with too many metaphors and similes. That's what I did, and the story got lost among wonderful metaphors and glowing descriptions. Even though they were beautiful, I had to cut masses of them out (I used them in subsequent books) so readers could follow the story.

Just get the story down.

Good writing communicates clearly, so that should be your only aim. You want the reader to be able to understand and follow your story. Don't feel that your writing should be any particular way. Simple is good, but if you naturally write in complex sentences with lots of embellishments, then let that flow. It's not wrong unless it's not your natural style, and you're trying to write like someone else or to fulfill some idea of what good writing is. The danger is in trying too hard. Remember that we want your voice to come out, and that will come out in your natural writing style. If you try too hard, you will thwart the very thing you most need to do—developing your own voice.

Write Every Day

King suggests that once you start on a book, you should write every day and complete the first draft in three months. Why? To keep it all flowing and not lose the impetus and creative juice. If we have a full-time job, we might be stretched to complete it in three months, but aim for no more than four.

'Once I start work on a project, I don't stop, and I don't slow down unless I absolutely have to,' says King. 'If I don't write every day, the characters begin to stale off in my mind ... I begin to lose my hold on the story's plot and pace.'

When the First Draft is Complete

Celebrate. It's quite a feat to finish a first draft. Even though it's only the start of your journey to publication, it warrants a pat on the back and a special dinner.

Then tuck it away somewhere out of sight where you won't be tempted to look at it, and leave it alone for at least six weeks. If you look at it straight away, it will look perfect to you, but it won't be perfect. If you have a break, then when you come back to it, you'll be much more able to see it objectively and see what needs to be done to improve it.

It's after the first draft that your knowledge of writing craft becomes important, so if you've written your first draft and you haven't studied the topics in the next section of this book, then this is the time to do so. Then when you return to your book to do your second draft, you'll have a good basis for evaluating what you've written, and you'll have some idea of how to go about revising it.

PART THREE:
THE ELEMENTS OF
WRITING CRAFT

Do I Need to Know All This Before I Start?

You don't need to have studied the elements of writing craft before you write your first draft of your first book. I hadn't, and though it meant that I had to do a great deal of rewriting on that first book later, in some respects not knowing anything gave me a kind of freedom to simply write from my heart. My experience as an editor is that most people just start writing when they get inspired regardless of whether they know anything about writing or not, and the learning comes as part of their journey to publication. Working this way makes your learning relevant and effective because you have a project to which to apply it.

Of course, you can study it all before you start. Knowledge brings confidence that can help you get started. There is a lot to learn, though, and I feel that it's possible that if I'd studied it all before I started, I may have been so overwhelmed and so aware of all the things I could get wrong that I may never have started for fear of failure. I suspect that this is one of the reasons why many highly qualified editors have never written a book of their own. What's best for you is what's best for your own psychological makeup.

But it doesn't have to be an all-or-nothing situation. Since you've picked up this book, I think we can assume that, regardless of where you are in your writing journey, it's time for you to do some study on the craft of writing.

I suggest you write at least several chapters before studying the rest of this section. That will give you something to which to apply your learning.

Your understanding of the elements that make good writing really comes into play when you revisit your first draft and discover that something isn't working. Your knowledge will tell you what kinds of things you need to look at, teach you how to recognise what the problems are, and give you some idea of how to go about fixing the issues.

If you do read this section before writing your first draft, then leave enough time between studying this information and beginning to write so you can write without actively thinking about it.

The Importance of the Inciting Incident in Story Development

As a writer, I have always been fascinated by the power of storytelling. Whether it's a gripping novel, a captivating movie or an engaging TV series, a well-crafted story can transport us to different worlds, evoke emotions and leave a lasting impact. But have you ever wondered what makes a story truly compelling? One key element that plays a crucial role in story development is the inciting incident.

What is the Inciting Incident?

The inciting incident is the event or situation that sets the entire story in motion. It's the catalyst that disrupts the protagonist's ordinary world and forces them to embark on a journey of change and growth. This pivotal moment happens near the beginning of a story and serves as the trigger for the main conflict. Without a strong and well-executed inciting incident, a story may lack the necessary intrigue and fail to captivate the reader.

The Role of the Inciting Incident

In today's fast-paced world, capturing the reader's attention from the very beginning is more important than ever. With countless distractions competing for our time and interest, it's essential to grab the reader's attention right from the start. The inciting incident serves this purpose by presenting a compelling and intriguing event that hooks the reader and makes them invested in the story.

A well-crafted inciting incident introduces a sense of urgency and raises questions in the reader's mind. It creates a desire to uncover what happens next and keeps them eagerly turning the pages. Whether it's a shocking revelation, a life-altering decision or a mysterious occurrence, the inciting incident must be significant enough to make the reader care about the protagonist's journey.

Questions to Ask When Developing the Inciting Incident

- What is the protagonist's ordinary world like before the inciting incident?
- What event or situation will disrupt their ordinary world and set the story in motion?
- How does the inciting incident relate to the main conflict of the story?
- What emotions or reactions do you want to evoke in the reader with the inciting incident?
- Does the inciting incident create a sense of urgency and make the reader eager to know what happens next?

By asking these questions, you can ensure that your inciting incident is well-aligned with the overall story and effectively captures the reader's attention.

How the Inciting Incident Sets the Stage for the Rest of the Story

The inciting incident is not just a stand-alone event; it sets the stage for the rest of the story. It establishes the initial conflict, introduces key characters, and lays the groundwork for the protagonist's journey. The choices and actions taken by the protagonist in response to the inciting incident shape the entire storyline.

Furthermore, the inciting incident often foreshadows the challenges and obstacles the protagonist will face throughout the story. It creates a ripple effect that propels the narrative forward and creates a sense of anticipation in the reader. A well-crafted inciting incident sets the tone and direction for the entire story.

Common Mistakes to Avoid

While the inciting incident is a powerful tool for story development, there are some common mistakes that writers should be aware of and avoid.

One such mistake is making the inciting incident too predictable or cliché. If the reader can anticipate the inciting incident from a mile away, it loses its impact and fails to capture their attention.

Another mistake is placing it too soon or too late. The inciting incident doesn't happen in the first paragraph because the central character and their world need to be established first. Its placement in a novel should ideally occur within the first 10%–15% of the story's length. This allows enough time to establish the protagonist's normal world and character, but also ensures the story quickly launches into its central conflict. Don't confuse it with the first plot point, which should come after the inciting incident at around the 25% mark.

Another mistake is making the inciting incident too disconnected from the rest of the story. It should not be an isolated event that has no bearing on the protagonist's journey or the main conflict. The inciting incident should seamlessly integrate with the overall storyline and propel the narrative forward.

Lastly, it is important to avoid making the inciting incident too overwhelming or confusing. While it should be significant enough to create intrigue, it should not bombard the reader with too much information or leave them feeling lost. Striking the right balance is key to crafting a compelling inciting incident.

Techniques for Crafting a Compelling Inciting Incident

- **Start with a bang**: Make it a high-impact event or revelation that grabs the reader's attention.
- **Create conflict**: Introduce a conflict or dilemma that forces the protagonist to make a choice or take action.
- **Use foreshadowing**: Hint at the inciting incident before it happens, building suspense and anticipation.
- **Evoke emotion**: Make the inciting incident emotionally charged to create a strong connection between the reader and the protagonist.
- **Make it relevant**: Ensure that the inciting incident is directly tied to the main conflict and has a meaningful impact on the protagonist's journey.

Examples of Successful Inciting Incidents in Popular Stories

- In J K Rowling's *Harry Potter and the Philosopher's Stone* (*Harry Potter and the Sorcerer's Stone* in the US), the inciting incident occurs when Harry receives his acceptance letter to Hogwarts School of Witchcraft and Wizardry. This event disrupts his ordinary world and thrusts him into a world of magic and adventure.

- In *The Hunger Games* by Suzanne Collins, the inciting incident takes place when Katniss volunteers as a tribute in place of her younger sister, Prim. This decision sets in motion the deadly competition and forces Katniss to fight for her life.

- In the movie *The Matrix,* the inciting incident occurs when Neo is contacted by the mysterious hacker Morpheus. This event leads Neo to question the nature of reality and ultimately join the fight against the machines.

Deepening Point of View

When writing a novel, which point of view you're going to use is one of the first things you should decide on. Why? Because it sets your whole approach to writing the story, and if your point of view isn't consistent, and changes between points of view aren't clear, you confuse the reader. They won't know who is telling the story.

When an author isn't clear about their point of view, they tend to end up with the point of view bouncing around all over the place. Readers who recognise this will realise that they can't trust this author to deliver a good story, and so they'll simply stop reading. No one wants to waste their time on an author they suspect doesn't know what they're doing. General readers may not be able to say what's wrong, but something will feel 'off'.

Even subtle point-of-view confusion weakens your writing. A great story will forgive many mistakes, but if you want to develop real skill as an author, and you want to produce a truly professional product, point of view is something you need to get right.

First-person point of view is easy to recognise and write; the place where confusion is rife is in the difference between third-person intimate and third-person omniscient.

Third-person Confusions

Because omniscient point of view and third-person intimate are both third-person viewpoints— using 'he' or 'she' as the pronoun—they are easily confused. Also, both POVs can—and often do— appear in the same book. Once you're clear on the difference, you'll be better able to transition smoothly from one POV to another.

Omniscient POV

The omniscient version of third person is when the story is told by a narrator who knows everything about the story and about the people. Yes, they do know the thoughts of all the characters, but—and this is the key point—they do not write as if they *are* any of the characters. The narrator is a separate storyteller, *outside* of the characters and outside of the story. They do not see the world through any of the characters' eyes. They see the story from their own perspective, from outside a character's mind and body, not from within a character's mind and body.

Though it's not fashionable these days, the omniscient point of view also allows the narrator to make a commentary on the story, to give their opinion on the events and characters, something you never do in a book with third-person intimate sections in it, as it would intrude upon the story.

The point that arouses confusion here is that the omniscient narrator knows the characters' thoughts and feelings, and some authors assume that this means they can reveal any and every character's thoughts at any time. Some say that you cannot head hop in omniscient POV because the narrator isn't inside the character's head, but even if the writing is truly in omniscient POV, revealing several characters' thoughts in quick succession— sentence by sentence or paragraph by paragraph— and going back and forth from one to another is still head hopping. The writing is not as strong as keeping the focus on one person before moving to someone else. There are much stronger ways of telling a story than flipping through the thoughts and emotions of everyone in a scene.

Third-Person Intimate

In third-person intimate POV, the story is told from the point of view of one or more of the characters in the story. The narrator talks in the character's voice, not in the voice of an external viewer who is personally uninvolved in the action. The character refers to themselves in third person, using 'she' or 'he', but they share what that character is seeing, thinking, feeling, tasting and experiencing from the inside out.

The Difference

An omniscient narrator might say:

Kathryn gasped at the sight of Joshua and Celia kissing on the garden bench in a blatant display of passion. The sweet scent from the jasmine on the trellis wafted over the scene, mocking the bitterness Kathryn felt at his betrayal. She wondered if he even cared that she might come upon them. Tears welled in her eyes, breaking through her usual composure, and she ran from the sight, stifling her sobs. Once out of hearing, she stopped and, drying her tears, decided that she would not allow him to make a fool out of her. She was determined to plot her revenge, wait until the time was right, and then make him pay for his sins.

From the intimate perspective of Kathryn, who doesn't know the name of the flowers, the narration would be something like:

Kathryn gasped. Joshua, the two-timing bastard, was blatantly snogging Celia on the garden bench. Her stomach soured at the hot and heavy display. Didn't he give a damn that she might come across them? The sweet scent from the little white flowers that wafted over the sickening scene mocked the bitterness lodging like a rock in her heart at his betrayal. Tears rose and burst through her self-control. She turned and fled, stifling her sobs until she was out of hearing range. She'd bide her time, but she'd get her revenge, make him pay for his sins. No one makes a fool out of Kathryn O'Dowd!

Note how the first example is written from the view of someone watching from outside Kathryn and in a voice unaffected by the scene. The narrator is simply telling the story; he or she is not involved in it. The narrator does know what Kathryn is thinking and feeling, but he or she doesn't refer to how the emotion feels in her body—that's the realm of the intimate point of view. The omniscient narrator notes that she feels a certain way—as in 'the bitterness Kathryn felt'—but not how that emotion feels to her or how it manifests in her body—as in 'the bitterness lodging like a rock in her heart', and 'her stomach soured ...'

The omniscient narrator also shares Kathryn's thoughts—as in 'she wondered if ...' and 'she decided ...' and 'she was determined ...' But in the intimate view, we have Kathryn's direct thoughts—as in, 'Didn't he give a damn ...' and, 'She'd bide her time, but she'd get her revenge. No one makes a fool out of Kathryn O'Dowd!' These are things she actually thinks, only she's using third person, not first person.

The language in the intimate example is the kind of language that Kathryn would use. It's written in her voice. It uses the kinds of words she would use to describe the scene, which deepens the characterisation and is more indicative of how she feels, hence 'intimate'—for example: 'snogging' instead of 'kissing'; 'hot and heavy display' instead of 'passionate'; 'little white flowers' instead of 'jasmine'; 'sickening scene' instead of just 'scene'; the addition of 'like a rock in her heart'; and she refers to her 'self-control' rather than 'usual composure'.

How to Write in Third-Person Intimate

Put yourself in the story. Pretend you are the character, and you're telling the story from their perspective. Place yourself in the scene, and describe what you (as the character) see, hear, smell, taste and so on. Be that person in your imagination. Live the scene from inside your character's mind and tell the story as if you are them.

If you find that referring to yourself as 'she' or 'he' makes doing that too difficult, then start by writing in first person. Have your character tell the story using 'I', 'me' and 'mine', and then change it to third person afterwards.

For example, I might write:

I stared out the window at the darkening sky. My heart seemed to skip a beat with every flash of lightning and crash of thunder.

Tension tightened my brow, threatening a headache. Will George make it home before the roads become impassable? I couldn't bear the thought of him being caught between rapidly rising streams.

In third person it becomes:

She stared out the window at the darkening sky. Her heart seemed to skip a beat with every flash of lightning and crash of thunder. Tension tightened her brow, threatening a headache. Would George make it home before the roads became impassable? She couldn't bear the thought of him being caught between rapidly rising streams.

In third-person intimate POV, your POV character is telling the story through their eyes, using their language, and giving their perspective, but they can *only* say what they know, see, hear, taste, feel or assume. They cannot write about their own physical appearance as it would look from the outside—unless they're looking in a mirror— nor can they write what someone else is thinking or feeling—unless they're telepathic! They can, however, describe another character's expression, gestures and tone of voice in a way that gives one an idea of what they might be thinking or feeling. Examples:

- They can feel their face flush or heat, but they can't see that their face has turned red.
- They cannot use someone's name if they haven't yet been introduced to them by name.
- They can't talk about something that is around the corner if they have never been in that place before, nor can they know what's on a menu before they read it if they've never been to that restaurant before.
- They can't say that another character 'felt' angry or that their 'stomach churned with anger', but they can describe how that character 'stomped across the floor with a thunderous expression'.
- They can say that someone looked thoughtful and can conjecture as to what they might be thinking, but they can't say exactly what they're thinking. They can only say what they are thinking and feeling themselves. If you want to go inside the head of another character, it's time to change POV with either a section break or a smooth batten change—see below.
- They don't know what is going to happen in the future, and they only know what they have experienced in the past and what others have

told them.

- They don't know what they missed. So you can't say that they 'didn't see' someone look their way. If they didn't see it, they don't know about it.

POV Transitions

When using third-person intimate POV with more than one POV character, how we change from one character's POV to another's is important. This is where, if we don't make the change clear, and if the changes come often, flipping from one character to another and back again is called head hopping. Head hopping is considered unskilful writing because readers get confused as to who's telling the story.

The easiest and clearest way to make a smooth transition from one POV to another is to change POV at the start of a chapter or at the beginning of a change of scene, after a scene break.

It is also acceptable to make a section break within a scene and start the next section with the name of the new POV character in the first sentence and say what s/he's feeling or thinking. Even with section breaks, however, it's important not to have lots of little sections in different POVs.

Try to stay with one character's POV for as long as possible.

If you find that making a section break affects the flow of your story, you can also change POVs smoothly within scenes without a section break, but this is harder to do well. Refer to my book *The Elements of Active Prose: Writing Tips to Make Your Prose Shine* for more detail on ways to change points of view without head hopping.

Summary

Once you understand the difference between third-person POVs, writing in omniscient POV may seem terribly dull in comparison to writing in third-person intimate. Only in very skilled hands does omniscient POV compete well with the liveliness and deep characterisation of the intimate POV.

True omniscient POV cannot use the language/voice of any of the characters—except in dialogue—because the omniscient narrator has their own voice. An omniscient narrator can only express characters' thoughts by saying that a character 'thought', 'felt', 'wished', 'observed', 'determined', 'decided' and so on.

A helpful thing to remember for omniscient writing is that if the story is told well enough from outside, then what a character is thinking is clear by their actions, body language, gestures and expressions, so it's not necessary to look inside the character's mind. And when you do need to share what a character is thinking, make sure you don't then pop straight over to say what someone else is thinking. Stick with one character's thoughts for at least a few paragraphs before letting the reader know what someone else is thinking. That way, if you do get a bit too intimate in your writing, you'll not be giving the reader whiplash.

Character Development: Arcs and Journeys

I talked earlier about writing characters readers care about, but in addition to having well-fleshed-out, three-dimensional characters, they need to grow from the events in the story. Character development refers to the process of building and evolving your characters as your story unfolds. It involves creating distinct personalities, backgrounds and motivations that shape their actions, reactions and decisions throughout the narrative. A well-developed character will have a unique voice, showcase growth or change, and evoke an emotional response from the reader.

But character development is not just about creating a list of traits, quirks and physical attributes, or even about having a detailed backstory. It delves deeper into understanding the

174

character's desires, fears and beliefs that drive their actions and decisions. A well-rounded character will demonstrate consistency in their behaviour while also showcasing transformations and growth as they face challenges and conflicts.

Inner and Outer Journeys

Characters undergo both inner and outer journeys throughout a story. The outer journey is the series of physical challenges, obstacles and external conflicts a character encounters throughout the story. This journey typically serves as the catalyst for the character's inner journey, pushing them to confront their internal issues.

The inner journey is the emotional and psychological journey a character experiences as they pursue their goals and face conflicts. This journey often involves overcoming internal struggles, such as fears, doubts and flawed beliefs, which can lead to personal growth or change.

By intertwining the inner and outer journeys of your characters, you create a richer and more compelling narrative that resonates with your readers on a deeper level.

Character Arcs

The term 'character arc' refers to the transformation a character undergoes throughout a story from where they are emotionally, morally or spiritually at the start of the story to where they are at the end. Their transformation is often marked by a change in the character's beliefs, values or behaviour that comes about in response to their inner journey.

Positive Change

A positive-change character arc involves the protagonist overcoming external obstacles and internal flaws to become a better person. This type of arc is common in the hero's journey story structure and typically follows three key points:

- **The goal**: The character's initial aim or desire.
- **The lie**: A deeply rooted misconception the character has about themselves or the world, which hinders their progress.
- **The truth**: The character eventually overcomes the lie and embraces the truth, leading to self-improvement and the achievement of their goal.

Negative Change

A negative-change character arc depicts a character's downward spiral, either due to their internal struggles or the harsh circumstances they face. This type of arc can be powerful and moving, providing a realistic portrayal of human vulnerability. A negative character arc has the same three elements as in a positive arc—the goal, the lie and the truth—but the character reacts to them differently:

- **The goal**: The character's initial aim or desire.
- **The lie**: The character embraces the lie, believing it will lead to a positive outcome.
- **The truth**: The character ultimately realises that the lie has brought about negative consequences and self-destruction.

Character Development Through Relationships

Characters' relationships with one another can significantly impact their development and growth. These relationships can serve as sources of support, conflict or transformation, allowing your characters to evolve and change as they interact with others.

Allies and mentors are characters who help your protagonist on their journey, providing guidance, support or resources. These characters can reveal your protagonist's strengths and weaknesses, help them overcome obstacles and contribute to their growth or change.

Antagonists and rivals are characters who oppose or compete with your protagonist, creating conflict and challenges that drive the story forward. These characters can push your protagonist to confront their flaws, adapt to new situations and grow or change as a result.

Character Development Exercises

Create Character Profiles

Develop detailed profiles for your characters, including their physical attributes, personality traits, backstory, desires, fears and beliefs. This will give you a deeper understanding of your characters and help you depict their growth and change throughout the story.

Explore Relationships

Examine the relationships between your characters, considering how they impact each other's development and growth. Look for opportunities to create conflicts, alliances and mentors who challenge and support your characters on their journeys.

Map Out Character Arcs

Outline the character arcs for your main characters, including their initial goals, conflicts and resolutions. Consider how these arcs intertwine with the overall plot and contribute to the story's themes and messages.

Experiment with Different Character Arcs

Try writing different versions of your characters' arcs, exploring positive and negative change, as well as different types of conflicts and resolutions. This will help you gain a deeper understanding of character development and create more dynamic and engaging characters.

179

Analyse Well-Developed Characters

Study the character development of characters in books, films and other stories that resonate with you. Analyse how these characters grow and change throughout the narrative, and consider what techniques you can apply to your own writing.

Seek Feedback

Share your character development with others, such as writing groups, friends or mentors. Listen to their feedback and suggestions, and use this input to refine and improve your character development skills.

Practice Makes Perfect

Continue to practise character development by writing short stories, character sketches or scenes that focus on your characters' growth and change. The more you practise, the more comfortable and skilled you will become at crafting complex and engaging character arcs.

Mastering Dramatic Tension in Your Novel

In the world of storytelling, dramatic tension is the lifeblood that keeps readers turning the pages. It pulls them into the story, makes them care about the characters and keeps them guessing about what will happen next. Whether you're writing a thriller, a romance or an epic fantasy, creating and maintaining dramatic tension is crucial. Conflict isn't the only element that creates tension; humour, relationship dynamics, surprise and mystery also contribute to dramatic tension.

Different Types of Dramatic Tension

- **Conflict:** The most direct form of tension, involving a clash between characters, forces or within a character.
- **Humour:** While not traditionally associated with tension, humour can break tension or create its own form of suspense as readers anticipate a punchline or resolution.
- **Relationships:** Tension arising from interpersonal relationships, whether romantic, familial or platonic. This tension often stems from misunderstandings, unspoken feelings or opposing goals.
- **Surprise:** Unpredictability in the story that shocks or catches readers off guard, adding excitement and momentum.
- **Mystery:** The tension of the unknown, where readers and characters alike seek answers to compelling questions. This can be the core of a plot or a secondary element that adds depth.

By weaving these elements into your story, you create a rich tapestry of tension that keeps readers emotionally invested and eager for more. The key to maintaining dramatic tension is to balance these elements, ensuring they work together to support the story's central conflict and emotional journey.

How to Create Dramatic Tension in Your Writing

Though the following points relate closely to your basic plot elements, they aren't just applicable to the overall story, but also to every scene within it.

Establish Clear Stakes

To engage your readers, clearly define what's at risk for your protagonist. The stakes should be high enough to matter, whether it's a life-or-death situation, a critical relationship or an internal struggle. For instance, in a fantasy novel, the stakes might involve saving a kingdom; while in a romance, they could revolve around winning or losing true love. Make sure your readers understand what the protagonist stands to gain or lose, as this investment will keep them emotionally engaged.

Introduce Obstacles

Obstacles are the cornerstone of dramatic tension. They force your characters to confront challenges, adapt and make difficult choices. These obstacles can come in many forms: external conflicts like antagonists or dangerous environments, or internal struggles like fear or doubt. By placing these hurdles in the protagonist's path, you create a sense of uncertainty about whether they will achieve their goals, keeping readers hooked.

Create Internal Conflict

Internal conflict adds depth to your characters and enhances the story's emotional resonance. It involves the character's internal struggles, such as moral dilemmas, conflicting desires, or personal weaknesses. For example, a character might grapple with the decision to lie for a good cause or to stay true to their principles. This type of tension not only enriches the character but also adds layers to the narrative, making it more compelling.

Use Subplots

Subplots are secondary storylines that add complexity to your novel. They can introduce new characters, settings or conflicts that interact with the main plot, enriching the overall narrative. Subplots can also create additional tension, as they often come with their own stakes and obstacles. For instance, a subplot involving a protagonist's troubled relationship with a sibling can parallel and contrast with the main plot's themes, offering different perspectives and keeping the reader engaged.

Vary the Intensity

To keep your story dynamic, vary the intensity of the tension. While constant high tension can exhaust readers, a well-timed quiet moment can deepen their emotional connection to the characters. Alternate between high-stakes action scenes and more introspective, character-driven moments. This ebb and flow will not only prevent reader fatigue but also make the moments of high tension more impactful.

Surprise Your Reader

Unexpected twists and turns can be one of the most exciting aspects of a novel. Surprises keep readers on their toes and make them eager to find out what happens next. However, these twists should feel organic to the story and not contrived. Build up to them subtly, using foreshadowing and red herrings, so that when the twist arrives, it feels both surprising and inevitable.

Showing and Telling

You may have heard people say, 'Show, don't tell your story.' Following this advice is crucial for creating a compelling novel because showing the story brings it to life. If you're telling rather than showing your story, you're not drawing the reader into the story, so it simply doesn't have the same impact. I go into this in detail in my book *The Elements of Active Prose: Writing Tips to Make Your Prose Shine*, but here are the key points.

'Show, don't tell' means exactly what it says. You use descriptive, active language to show the story so the reader can see the scenes unfolding around them, rather than tell the story as if the reader is listening to a story being told. It is, of course, quite possible to tell a story in an engaging way, and talented authors can do this, but showing it makes it easier to create an immersive experience such that the reader feels as if they're right there in the scene, seeing the events for themselves.

For instance, telling says, 'George was angry.' Showing says, 'George stomped across the room, his hands clenched into fists.'

That way, you've shown the reader what was happening in the scene and let the reader see it for themselves, rather than telling them what the narrator concluded from the action—in this case, that George was angry.

If you tell a story rather than show it, the reader is passive and uninvolved, and that reader experience doesn't compete so well with movies, TV and video games.

Telling is also called expositional or expository prose because you're explaining something. This is what you do when you're writing an essay, and you don't want your novel to sound like an essay. Telling is fine in nonfiction, but in fiction you need to create vivid scenes so your readers are immersed in the story.

To show rather than tell, imagine yourself in the scene and describe what it's like there, what people are doing, what you're feeling (as the character) and what your senses are picking up on—sight, sound, touch, taste and smell. You describe how the world feels to the characters, so the reader can feel those sensations themselves. It's all about bringing the scenes to life in a very immediate way.

First drafts often have a lot of telling in them, and that's fine because the aim of the first draft is just to get the story down. We refine our approach at the revision and editing stage. But we don't need to show *all* the story. Some aspects of the story are better told—like transitions or secondary scenes where showing would give the scene too much emphasis for its role in the plot. Striking the right balance between showing and telling is crucial for maintaining a captivating narrative. Here are some tips for balancing show and tell in your novel:

- **Show emotions and reactions**: Rather than stating a character's emotions, show them through their actions, body language and dialogue.
- **Tell backstory and exposition**: Use telling to convey necessary background information or exposition, but avoid info dumps and weave the details seamlessly into your narrative.
- **Show important scenes**: When a scene is crucial to your plot or character development, show it in detail, allowing your reader to

experience it alongside your characters.

- **Tell transitions**: Use telling to bridge gaps in time or location, summarising events that aren't essential to the plot.
- **Vary your approach**: Mix showing and telling throughout your novel, balancing immersive scenes with informative passages.

We need to be able to recognise where we're telling, so we can change it if necessary. And since active prose is prose that shows rather than tells, studying what makes prose active rather than passive is a huge help in recognising when you've told a scene. Once you know what to look for, you'll be able to see exactly where your writing has headed into the telling side of things. My book *The Elements of Active Prose: Writing Tips to Make Your Prose Shine* gives you the knowledge you need to easily turn a told passage into a shown one.

Writing Dialogue

Writing dialogue well is an important skill for novelists because it adds to characterisation and drives much of the story. Stilted or unnatural-sounding dialogue is something readers will quickly notice, and they'll also quickly put your book down.

The important thing to understand about writing dialogue is that we don't speak the same way we write. Written English and spoken English are different. We have to write our dialogue as spoken English—in the way that people actually speak—but at the same time, we need to prune it back a bit. No one wants to read lots of 'well's and 'um's and all the little things people say in introductions, like, 'Lovely weather we're having, isn't it?' In a novel, we want the dialogue to be on point, not to wander off into general chattiness.

Start by writing exactly what your characters

might say, and then cut anything that doesn't move the story forward. I always read dialogue out loud, so I know if it sounds natural or not.

Essential Points

- **Ground your dialogue**: Occasionally, include facial expressions, gestures and body movement—such as tapping a foot to show impatience—and interactions with the setting—such as picking a coffee cup up from a table.
- **Vary the structure**: Break up long stretches of dialogue with action, description or internal thoughts to maintain a dynamic pace.
- **Stick to simple dialogue tags**: Use 'said', 'asked' and 'replied' with the occasional 'shouted' and 'yelled'. 'Said' goes unnoticed. Replacement words for said—also known as 'fancy tags'—such as 'remarked', 'commanded', 'agreed', 'argued' and so on stick out. Fancy tags distract the reader from the reading experience. They remind the reader that they're reading and thus take them out of the story. That's the very opposite of what you want. There are more skilful ways to avoid overusing 'said'.
- **Cut unnecessary tags**: Readers must know

who is saying what. However, your desire to make sure that the reader knows who's speaking shouldn't always result in a dialogue tag. You can cut dialogue tags completely where it's obvious who's speaking, such as where the speaker does an action before or after what they say. The action is sufficient to tell the reader who's speaking if you use the character's name or pronoun as the subject of the action. For example: Rose picked up the apple. 'I can't believe John has gone to Perth.' We know Rose is speaking because of her action in the previous sentence.

- **Write how people speak**: Write dialogue that sounds like real conversation, avoiding overly formal or stilted language. People often talk in short sentences, phrases and fragments, rather than in long sentences with big words, so write your dialogue the way they speak. Modern people also use contractions often. They are much more likely to say 'I'm' than 'I am'. Read your dialogue out loud to see if it sounds natural.

- **Reveal character**: Use dialogue to showcase your characters' personalities, emotions and relationships.

- **Use subtext**: People don't say everything they

think. In dialogue, less is often more, and it's usually more realistic. You can use characters' expressions, actions and gestures not only to ground the dialogue but also as subtext to communicate how they 'really' feel about the conversation. People sometimes say one thing and think another, and body language can indicate what they really think. Noting this kind of detail creates subtext in the dialogue, and that makes it interesting and real. You're conveying meaning through what your characters don't say, using body language, tone and context to provide depth and nuance.

- **Avoid info dumps**: Use dialogue to convey information, but avoid having characters recite large amounts of exposition.
- **Advance the plot**: Ensure your dialogue contributes to the story's progression, either by revealing information, creating conflict or prompting action.
- **Don't use actions as dialogue tags**: Sniffed, sobbed, smiled, beamed, laughed and so on are not dialogue tags; they are actions, so make sure there is a period and capital letter after the dialogue in such cases. For example: 'Troy is being horrible to me.' Jane sobbed.

Paragraph Breaks

Make sure you put paragraph breaks in the correct place. Doing so makes it clear to the reader which character is doing or saying what, and that minimises the number of dialogue tags you need to use. A break comes *after* a character has both acted and spoken and *before* the next character acts and/or speaks. Don't separate the character's action from their speech. For example:

> *Mary gasped at the sight before her.*
> *'Have you lost your mind, George? Running around dressed like that? What will people think?'*
> *George blinked. Was she serious or not? He cleared his throat.*
> *'No, Mary. I am quite sane.'*
> *'Really.'*
> *Mary chuckled like an impish schoolgirl.*
> *'That hat alone makes me wonder.'*
> *She folded her arms over her ample bosom.*
> *George harrumphed.*
> *'If one is going to a Halloween party, one should dress appropriately. I am in a costume; therefore, I am dressed appropriately.'*

George raised his eyebrows, daring her to challenge that.

'Do you not think this suitable for such an event?'

Mary cocked her head and appraised him again.

'Well, I suppose a grinning gooseberry makes as good a Halloween hat as any.'

These are the correct paragraph breaks for this passage:

Mary gasped at the sight before her. 'Have you lost your mind, George? Running around dressed like that? What will people think?'

George blinked. Was she serious or not? He cleared his throat. 'No, Mary. I am quite sane.'

'Really.' Mary chuckled like an impish schoolgirl. 'That hat alone makes me wonder.' She folded her arms over her ample bosom.

George harrumphed. 'If one is going to a Halloween party, one should dress appropriately. I am in a costume; therefore, I am dressed appropriately.' He raised his eyebrows, daring her to challenge that. 'Do you not think this suitable for such an event?'

Mary cocked her head and appraised him again. 'Well, I suppose a grinning gooseberry makes as good a Halloween hat as any.'

Backstory and Information Delivery: What to Avoid

Writing backstory into a novel or delivering information in an effective way can be challenging. It's important not to fall into one of the following mistakes.

Too Much Information

Generally, the reader needs less information than you think they do. So go through the information you have about characters, events and the world in which the events take place, and cut out anything that doesn't directly impact on the present story. Only include information such as backstory or worldbuilding elements in a scene if the scene cannot be understood without it. Sometimes the elaborate backstory—or parts of it—that we've created has no direct impact on the events in the story, in which case, there's no need to include the information at all. It has still played an important role, however, in that it helped us write our character and the events with a deeper understanding than we would have had we not constructed the backstory.

The author needs to know all the details of a character's background, but the reader only needs to know what is relevant to the story. For example, they don't need to know what kind of school a character went to unless something happened during their time there that directly influences their actions in the story. Readers are quite capable of making assumptions about characters' pasts from what they do or say now. There is no reason to lay out all the details for them.

Sometimes something has happened in the past that sets the scene for the present story, and you want to include it as backstory—a scene from the past set into the present story. In general, avoid doing this, because backstory delivered this way can break the flow of the present story and slow the pace. Ask yourself if the information is necessary, and if it is, does it need to be delivered as a complete scene? Pertinent points could be included as a memory when a character has time for reflection.

Some novels are structured around one story thread set in the past and one set in the present, told consecutively. In such books, the story shifts from the past to the future and back, but this is not backstory; it is two different-but-related story arcs.

Info Dumps

The term info dump refers to any long segment of information—usually told, not shown—that feels to the reader as if the author has dumped all the information in there in one undigestible chunk. A good guideline for information delivery is no more than two paragraphs at the most.

Information dumps usually include too much information or information that's unnecessary or unrelated to the present events. The problem with information dumps is that they slow the story down and can even obscure the plot rather than illuminate it. On top of that, readers tend to skip them because they just want to know what comes next in the story, and that makes all those words pointless.

Poor Timing

Don't tell the reader everything about a character or place when you first introduce them to the reader. This is not only unnecessary but also tends to come across as an info dump, with all the issues that entails. Only tell the reader the pertinent points about a character or place *at the time when they need to know.*

If you decide that writing backstory into a scene is necessary, then be careful where you put it in the book structure. Placing backstory after a pause in the action works. Placing it in the middle of building tension is not a good idea, as readers will likely find it an annoying distraction from the main thrust of the story.

Telling Instead of Showing

How a character acts in a scene reveals their characteristics. There's no need to tell the reader that Joe is an avid sports fan, for instance, when you can show him teaching his child to play baseball or start a scene with him cheering on his favourite team—be it live or on TV. Characteristics should be shown through description of events as they unfold, not told to the reader.

If you want a reader to know about the cultural beliefs of a tribe, for instance, you don't need to tell the reader all about their religion; you simply show it in action. Instead of saying that a tribe 'worshipped the moon with blood sacrifices', you write a scene where their high priestess cuts the head off a chicken, while the rest of the group chants with their arms raised to the full moon.

Unrealistic Dialogue

No matter how you deliver it, an info dump is still an info dump, and having a character tell another character all the information will not disguise that fact unless you break it up and set it in a realistic conversation.

The first question you need to ask yourself is whether the character being told the information needs to know it or might already know it. Don't have a character tell another character things they would logically already know.

Be careful not to make a character suddenly sound like something out of a nonfiction book. Whatever information they deliver must be told in the character's voice, and for sure, they'll not give the same level of detail as you'd find in a history book.

Another mistake is delivering all the information in one monologue. Instead of having one character simply tell the other all the information, have one ask questions of the other or have them interrupt occasionally or ask for clarification, which then leads the person expounding to go deeper into their topic. This will make it much more natural.

One character could disagree with the other. The resulting tension as they argue their points is more interesting than a straight exposition. You could also have the first character give incorrect information that the second character could correct.

Adding these kinds of elements to dialogue that delivers information will make it much more interesting.

The Key Point on Backstory

Writing backstory should only be done if you can't find a more effective way to deliver the information. In my first book, *Lethal Inheritance,* I struggled with this and eventually decided that I didn't need any backstory written as a separate scene. The information I couldn't get across any other way became something the protagonist read in a book she'd been given to study—delivered one paragraph at a time at a point where she needed to find the information.

Working with Similes, Metaphors and Symbolism in Writing

Similes, metaphors and symbolism in writing are elements that flip writing over the line from ordinary writing to writing worthy of the literary label, meaning that it's the kind of writing that is valued for 'quality of form'.

Similes, metaphors and symbolism give depth to the writing by imbuing it with a deeper layer of meaning. These literary devices ignite the readers' imagination, making them engage with the writing in an active way, which increases their reading pleasure.

Symbolism

Symbolism is the use of symbolic images to represent ideas or qualities. An author who uses symbolism is using the indirect suggestion of symbols to express mystical ideas, emotions and states of mind.

Light quality and weather are often used as a symbol for a character's emotional state. A scene set in a storm has a very different emotional effect than one set on a sunny day. A character who is ruminating on how miserable their life is might stare out a window into a rainy day, and if it's sunny outside, then the sunshine could be used to make them feel even more miserable; they could see the bright, cheerful weather as mocking their misery.

Dim light makes things difficult to see, and we know from horror movies that darkness is scary. A ray of sunshine falling into a dim room is a powerful visual image of hope cutting through misery, as is a sunburst through clouds. The sky clearing of clouds can foreshadow a change in a character's life. Such symbolism can be used to underline a point or emotion—but be careful of overkill—or it can be used to add something that isn't spoken of in the narrative.

In the following excerpt from my novel

Stalking Shadows, I use a physical path to represent the psychological/spiritual path on which the protagonist travels. I have a full moon touching the path so that it shimmers, giving it a magical quality, and I use the word silver in the simile 'like a silver ribbon' to reinforce this sense of the special quality of this path. Comparing the path to a ribbon in the simile gives a sense that this path is something that has been wound out before the protagonist, ready for her to walk on and follow to the end.

> *Touched by the full moon, the path shimmered before them like a silver ribbon, and the mountain peak of shadowed crags and glistening snow rose like a beacon in the black sky over Minion Hills. Its ghostly presence reminded Ariel of her quest to seek and destroy the Master Demon that resided there.*

Describing the peak as shadowed crags and glistening snow is a symbol for the ups (glistening snow) and downs (shadowed crags) my protagonist has already been going through at this point; it's a reflection of how the self-doubt and fear she often feels contrasts with the hope and power she feels at other times. The simile 'like a beacon in the black sky' refers to the snowy peak and gives a sense of hope and direction. The last sentence is the protagonist relating to the symbolism to draw it out further.

Of course, a reader does not necessarily realise all this consciously as they read. The symbolism just gives them a rich visual image imbued with meaning.

Whole books can be symbolism. For instance, at the end of *The Life of Pi*, the reader wonders whether any of the events on the boat actually happened. We realise that the animals could simply be symbols for actual people whose behaviour reminded the narrator of animals.

Similes

Similes are the easy ones to recognise and understand. In the example above, saying that the path is 'like a silver ribbon' and the peak is 'like a beacon' are similes. Similes say that something is 'like' something else.

Metaphors

A metaphor is a figure of speech in which a word or phrase is applied to an object or action to which it is not literally applicable. It can also be a thing regarded as representative or symbolic of something else.

A metaphor is different to a simile because a simile says that something is 'like' something else, whereas a metaphor directly compares two things as if they are the same.

> *'My lips, two blushing pilgrims, ready stand to smooth that rough touch with a tender kiss.'*
> - William Shakespeare, Romeo and Juliet.

The lips are not really two blushing pilgrims, but describing them this way gives a sense of the chasteness of the moment. If you write that a character 'filled the room with sunshine' that's a metaphor, as is saying their 'voice dripped honey' or that they had 'eyes of velvet'. The simile version would be saying that their eyes were 'like' velvet or their voice sounded sweet and smooth 'like' honey. But whether metaphor or simile, both add interest to your writing by painting a visual picture that ignites the reader's imagination.

Extended Metaphors

Magical realism is a genre that extends metaphors into whole scenes. A character may enter a scene written as if it occurred in the main narrative, but the occurrence is actually an extended metaphor for a purely psychological narrative.

I do this in my young-adult novel *You Can't Shatter Me*, where whole scenes are metaphors. For example, in one scene the male protagonist experiences letters attacking him—a symbol for his frustration at school. In another, he uses a battering ram to break up the concrete encasing his feet—a symbol for him consciously breaking habits and beliefs that are holding him back.

I don't recommend using extended metaphors unless you're writing magical realism because readers would find extended metaphors confusing in a book that is not magical realism in style.

What to Avoid

Don't Overdo the Similes and Metaphors

I made this mistake in the first draft of my first book, and though the similes and metaphors made for rich symbolism, they slowed down the action. The reader had to read slowly to digest the meaning and lost the story. I took out two of every three, so that the ones I left really shone out from the plainer language around them.

For us to be able to fully appreciate paintings on the wall, we need space between them. It's the same with metaphors and similes. If you naturally write with a lot of them in your first draft, that's fine, just don't add them in thinking that it will make your writing better. You can subtract excessive metaphors and similes at the second-draft stage, or you can add some in if your first draft is lacking in this area.

Don't Mix Your Metaphors

A mixed metaphor is a succession of incongruous or ludicrous comparisons, not recommended in general writing because they confuse the reader by sending mixed messages.

> *That's awfully thin gruel for the right wing to hang their hats on.*
> *The ball has been down this court before, and I can see already the light at the end of the tunnel.*

If you avoid more than one metaphor in a sentence, you'll avoid this. Alternatively, make sure that your metaphors in any one sentence refer to the same image. For example:

> *That's awfully thin gruel for the right wing to feed their campaign.*
> *The ball has been down this court before, but with a good wallop it'll be soaring over the fence in no time.*

How to Use Similes, Metaphors and Symbolism

Now that you know that these literary devices exist, they may naturally creep into your writing. I feel that if you immerse yourself in your story's world, as I've suggested previously, then you give yourself the best possible chance of metaphors, similes and symbolism appearing without your conscious participation. But if that doesn't happen, then there is plenty of time in later drafts to enrich your writing by adding some.

Writing Descriptions

Words ignite the reader's imagination. They form concepts and visual pictures in the reader's mind, and so knowing how to write descriptions is a vital skill for anyone writing a novel. Descriptions give the reader a full experience; they help make the reading immersive. Novels without description are barren, like a desert. They may still have their beauty from other aspects, such as riveting action, but they will lack the depth and fecundity of a landscape lush from rain.

Even a little description can add a great deal of flavour to your writing, especially if you write it so that it deepens characterisation and uses aspects of the character's sensory experience in a symbolic way. The lack of sensory cues means that I'm not pulled as deeply into the story as I am when the words paint a picture or, better still, flow through my mind with the vividness of a movie.

So descriptions are important, but there are some traps in writing descriptions that you can avoid and some pointers to set you in the right direction.

Don't Assume

Don't assume that the reader knows the setting. You need to set each scene with some description so the reader knows where the action is taking place. Books set in our Western world tend to have less description because the author assumes the reader knows what an office or a city street, for example, looks like, but city streets don't all look the same.

A filthy, garbage-strewn street adds flavour to a scene where the character is doing something underhand or illegal, whereas a clean street indicates a city that is cared for, and such an image could communicate a sense of safety or a fresh start. Old buildings creak, and their floors are not even, making the reader feel unsafe, but if the building is lovingly restored, they have a cosy, cared-for feeling. New buildings can feel sterile, which gives a hard edge, a sense of uncaring, or they can feel light and spacious. Old furniture can have individual character and aesthetic merit, or it can be dark and dull, scratched and an indication of poverty. It all depends on how you describe your setting, but if you don't describe it, you miss an opportunity to deepen your reader's experience, to make the reading of your book an immersive experience, and therefore a rich and rewarding one.

So don't assume that the reader can see the office or the street or the home where your scene takes place. This is particularly important if you're writing a fantasy world where everything is different to our own world. In this instance, you must create the world of your story with your descriptions.

Create Mood with Your Words

Look at this:

> *A wind kicked up, scattering the autumn leaves across the sidewalk and sending a chill down Tom's spine. A car screeched past with hard-rock music blaring, and a taxi splashed through a puddle full of icy water. Desperate to get to Sally's place before it was too late, Tom pushed through the crowd, frustrated at how they slowed his progress.*

This description gives a feeling of cold desperation with the words 'chill', 'icy', 'desperate' and 'frustrated'. Even the rock music adds to the feeling with its heart-pounding beat, screeching guitar and harsh voices. Autumn is a time of death and descent into darkness, and fallen autumn leaves are dead, so this also adds to the feeling.

The same street on a sunny day in summer would give a completely different feeling, so you aren't just describing a place, you're adding mood and feeling to your writing. The quality of the light in a scene is important; the way light falls on a character (sharp or soft), the colour (warm or cold), the general atmosphere of the environment (tense or relaxed) and the time of day all make the writing more evocative.

Use All the Senses

Don't just describe what is seen; include smells, tastes, sounds and touch as well. In our example, Tom feels a chill and hears the rock music, but he could also notice how the petrol fumes sully the fresh air. In this instance, the addition of the sense of smell is symbolic of how Sally's dilemma has sullied his pristine life.

That doesn't mean, of course, that every description must have all senses, just that you use different senses at different times to describe different things.

Putting yourself in a character's shoes, noticing what they would notice, is one way to encourage symbolism to emerge in your descriptions.

Add Character

A character's office or home tells us a lot about the character. What kind of furniture have they chosen? Do they have photos of their family on their desk? Are they messy or neat? A tidy office or home indicates a tidy mind, and a messy desk indicates a disorganised person, or perhaps someone with a unique filing system that could be pointed out as a quirk of the character.

When writing in a character's voice in first person or third-person intimate, what they notice and the language they use is particularly important for deepening character. Let's look at our example again. As written above, it's in the voice of a narrator, and that's fine, but what if you use the voice of the character?

A freezing wind scattered a bunch of wet leaves across the sidewalk—more stuff to wade through. As if he didn't have enough trouble already struggling through the

217

crowded sidewalk and fighting the chill that ran all the way down his spine. He hoped it wasn't a premonition of what he'd find when he finally got to Sally's place. He shoved past a girl giggling into her phone and shouldered a man out of his way, getting a curse in return. He didn't care. Sally needed him—now. A beat-up car screeched past with hideous music blaring—a perfect expression of his frustration. Should he take a taxi? One headed his way. He stepped closer to the road and waved it down, but the taxi didn't slow; it just splashed a puddle of icy water all over his shoe.

This version uses the character's voice. You still get a description of the scene, but seeing it from the character's point of view deepens the characterisation. This is not necessarily 'better' than the other version; both are good descriptions. Which approach you use depends on the point of view in which you're writing.

'What a character chooses to notice and how they describe it tell us a lot about them; a cheerful person is more likely to notice the sunshine than the shadows, for instance, but

when miserable, that same person would be more likely to dwell on the deep shadows in a room. A teen uses different language to an adult, and the words they use indicate not just what they're seeing but also how they feel about it. For example, what is a 'stunning Rueben's original' to the adult with the art history background is 'some kind of old picture' to the teen more interested in stealing the flat-screen TV. So your descriptions can deepen your characters.' From The Elements of Active Prose: Writing Tips to Make Your Prose Shine.

Make Your Descriptions Action Based.

Our example description is action based; things are happening to Tom as the scene is described. Unlike this version of the same place:

A wind blew autumn leaves across the sidewalk. The street was full of cars, taxis, and puddles of icy water, and people crowded the pavement. Would Tom get to Sally before it was too late?

219

Same scene, but the description is static and devoid of any reaction or involvement by Tom. The wind blew, which is some action, but it doesn't scatter leaves or send a chill down Tom's back. The cars, taxis and puddles are just there; they don't do anything. Description is much more interesting when it's tied into the action.

Don't Write Your Description in Chunks

A mistake I made in the first drafts of my first book was to write description in chunks of a couple of paragraphs at a time. Many beginning writers do the same, and some fantasy books, even famous ones, do it too. If they describe the scene in evocative language, it works okay for a lot of readers, but if you want to avoid impatient readers skipping your carefully crafted descriptions, then, regardless of the length, they are best written through the eyes of a character involved in the scene emotionally or actively.

Chunks of description that add nothing to the action or characterisation simply slow the story down. But why write descriptions in chunks when you can break up the blocks of description by inserting descriptions into the action?

Don't think of descriptions as something separate from the story. If you stop the action to give a paragraph or more of description, the reader who just wants to know what happens next will be tempted to skip it. Instead, write what the character notices while he or she is engaged in the action.

This example is from *Stalking Shadows*, book two of my *Diamond Peak* series:

> *Ariel and Nick crossed a muddy stream on conveniently placed rocks, wound around enormous clumps of granite, and climbed continually on a gentle grade. Ariel glanced back across the open landscape at the Observatory tower fading into the distance and wondered if she'd ever see the delightful Englishman and his manor again.*

Nick and Ariel are doing something. They are crossing, winding around and climbing. Ariel also looks back and wonders something. Also note the words that reflect Ariel's feelings about the landscape—'conveniently placed', 'enormous', 'gentle'.

Don't Overdo the Detail

Readers need enough description to give them an idea of the setting and what's happening, but don't fall into the trap of writing every action in detail, because that's not only unnecessary but also tedious. When a character boards a plane, for example, we don't need to know that he walks up the stairs, one foot after the other, with one hand on the railing and the other holding his cabin baggage. We all know how to get onto an aeroplane! However, if the character walks across the tarmac to get to the plane, that's an indication of a small or undeveloped airport and so is worthy of a mention.

The important thing is not to bog action scenes down with detailed description or thought processes. Some scenes need more description than others, of course, and that's one way to play with pacing—detailed descriptions slow the pace, so leave them out when speed is important.

Drop the 'Hads' and 'Withs'

Try to write your descriptions without using 'with', 'that' and 'had'. These words aren't very interesting and can make your descriptions clunky and, if overused, amateurish. We can't avoid these words entirely, and to do so would be unnatural and unnecessary. The point is to try not to rely on them. If you try to write descriptions without such words, you'll find your descriptions become more interesting and livelier.

Example:

Dull:

Sally was tall and had long, messy blonde hair with red streaks.

Lively:

Sally's blonde hair, streaked red, hung in rat tails around her shoulders. She towered over George.

Be Specific

Vague words like 'strange', 'something', 'handsome', 'beautiful' and so on don't really tell us much. For example, 'An eerie wheezing sound came from the kitchen' is better than 'A strange sound came from the kitchen'. And 'She noticed his long lashes, full lips and chiselled bone structure, and felt a little flutter in her chest' is better than 'She noticed how handsome he was'.

Being specific gives a much clearer visual image to the reader, which is the whole point of descriptions.

Crafting a Satisfying Ending

Be it happy, sad, bittersweet or even a bit of a cliffhanger, the important thing is that your ending leaves your reader satisfied. A terrible ending can ruin an otherwise good book. I have been known to throw a book at a wall and scream in frustration when that happens. That was back when I read paperbacks; I haven't thrown an ebook at the wall, but I have cursed the author and sworn not to buy another book of theirs, because I can't trust that they won't do the same in another book. And after spending hours on a story, I really need it to end in a satisfying way.

A 'satisfying' ending doesn't necessarily mean a happy ending, since you can have a happy ending that isn't satisfying—if it's unbelievable, for instance. Of course, romance readers expect a happy ending, so if you're writing romance, then a happy ending is what your readers will find satisfying. And mystery readers expect the central mystery to be solved, so for your ending to be satisfying, it must also take genre expectations into account.

But for all genres, a sense of closure is what's most important for a satisfying ending. You must ensure your protagonist's primary goal or conflict is resolved, whether they succeed or fail.

You also need to tie up loose ends in subplots or secondary conflicts. That doesn't mean that a problem or mystery in a subplot needs to be fully resolved, but it does have to be referred to, not forgotten or left hanging, so you either provide a resolution or hint at future developments.

You also need to show how your characters have changed and grown throughout the story. That's the inner journey I talked about previously. If the central character hasn't changed at all, your reader may be left wondering what the point of it all was.

The ending should also evoke some emotion, some emotional response from your reader, whether it's joy, sadness, hope, or surprise. I recommend not making your ending too bleak. Leave the reader with some hope, even if it's just a glimmer.

Some people love a tear-jerker, an ending

that makes them cry, and if your readers cry, then even though it won't be to everyone's taste, you do have a strong ending. Consider leaving some aspects of your story open to interpretation. That will encourage your readers to ponder and discuss your novel.

Cliffhangers

I'm personally not a fan of cliffhangers, but part of that is because they're rarely done well. Many of them aren't endings at all. The story just stops. That's not an ending, and calling it a cliffhanger doesn't make stopping the story without a conclusion okay. It's not okay because you've missed Act Three of the basic three-part structure—the conclusion.

You must give your reader some conclusion, even if you've left your protagonist in a sticky situation because there's a sequel; you still need to resolve the major story thread for that book—and show character development, tie up loose ends and evoke emotion.

A good series has an overarching plot or theme that isn't resolved until the last book, but each book in the series should have its own plot within that overarching plot, and the plot for each book should be resolved while leaving the overarching plot open until the end.

After the conclusion, you can add a little bit that leads into the next story that leaves the reader wanting to know how the protagonist gets out of that sticky situation. That's a skilfully done cliffhanger.

But be very careful if you're planning a cliffhanger, because if it's an obvious ploy to get readers to buy the next book, that can backfire. Readers don't like to feel they're being manipulated into buying the next book. I've read enough reviews to know that I'm not the only reader who will refuse to buy more in a series under those circumstances. Maybe think of a more subtle way to hook the reader into the sequel than risking a cliffhanger.

The essential tips for crafting a satisfying ending:

- **Resolve the main conflict**: Ensure your protagonist's primary goal or conflict is resolved, whether they succeed or fail.
- **Tie up loose ends**: Address any subplots or secondary conflicts, providing a resolution or hinting at future developments.
- **Show character growth**: Demonstrate how your characters have changed and grown throughout the story.
- **Evoke emotion**: Aim to evoke an emotional

response from your reader.

- **Leave room for interpretation**: Consider leaving some aspects of your story open to interpretation.

Should Authors Use AI in Their Writing?

The answer to this question is a personal one, and it depends on how we answer the following kinds of questions: Why do we write? What do we want to get out of it? What do we care most about when it comes to our writing? And ultimately, what brings us satisfaction in our writing? In the end, it boils down to the question of whether using AI to assist with our writing will help us achieve our aims and whether its use will increase, decrease or not affect the level of satisfaction we gain from our writing. Personal satisfaction is important in any art form. It's what keeps us doing it and what makes us feel good about what we produce.

If you wouldn't feel good about having used AI in your writing, then it's best you don't use it, but by the time you get to read this—power and water usage issues aside—a better question for most people might be 'How *much* should authors use AI in their writing?' or 'How *can* authors use AI in their writing and still call it their own writing?' I say this because as time goes by and authors experiment with what's available, many authors will discover that artificial intelligence large language models (LLM) are useful tools. It doesn't have to be an all-or-nothing decision, because you can use AI just to help you with specific tasks, not to write your whole book, so you can retain a sense of ownership over the result.

Creative Ownership Considerations

The issues around AI usage in the arts aren't as clearcut as many make them out to be. It's easy to fall into hard-line for-or-against positions without examining the finer points or being aware of the larger picture. Note that I am not advocating for or against AI usage in the arts here; I'm merely raising points pertinent to the discussion.

For instance, the idea that AI art or writing generators have 'stolen' all the works on which they have been trained misses the point that human training in the arts occurs in the same way. An artist goes to a gallery—without paying for admission or asking the artist before hand if they can view their work—and wanders around the gallery looking at a variety of works. They note how the artists use colour, form, movement, line, texture and so on to express different feelings and concepts, and then they go home and create a work that either consciously or unconsciously uses that information. But we don't call that stealing; we call that learning. It's the same with reading and writing. Our writing is influenced by every book we have ever read, particularly authors whose work we admire. And we may not have bought those books; we may have borrowed them from a library or a friend. We certainly do not own the rights to the books we've read, and yet—to a greater or lesser extent—they influence our writing. The difference between human and AI learning here is not in the *use* of the training material but in the huge *volume* of material used and in the AI's *technical ability and speed* in producing an artwork or story based on that learning.

Also, the idea of what constitutes creative 'ownership' isn't as clear cut as we might initially think.

Consider ghostwriters; they get no accreditation for the books they write on behalf of others. The person whose story they write—usually a famous person—is always listed as the author, and yet that 'author' never writes a single word of 'their' book. The ghost writer, who actually wrote the book, is not considered the author, or even mentioned in the credits, not even as a contributor. James Patterson gets other people to write his first drafts, based on his outlines, then he edits them afterwards. Is he the author or not? Only partly, but nevertheless, we regard him as the author, as the creator. If the ghost writer is an AI, does that—contrary to the accepted system of not crediting ghostwriters as authors—make the AI the author? And if so, what about the person who directed everything the AI wrote; are they not the author because they chose an AI to do their ghostwriting? Perhaps the ghostwriting system is wrong not to credit the ghost writer as the author or part author, but it shows how the publishing world, as it exists today, considers the role of a writing assistant in terms of ownership of the work.

Contrary to what some think, AI generators do not 'do it all for you'. They do not replace the author or the artist because they produce what *you* want in response to what *you* ask them to do. AI produces nothing by itself, and the results you get depend on how well you instruct it. Authors who use AI—

in whatever capacity—to help them produce their work still need the knowledge of writing contained in this book if they are to produce quality. They still need the creative vision to inspire a project and ensure the final product fulfills that vision. An AI doesn't come up with the concept for a book or the themes or how you want them handled. It needs instructions from the author every step of the way. In AI art, the quality comes not from traditional technical expertise, but from the creative vision of the artist. It's the same for writing. No matter how a book is written, it's the ideas behind the books that are important.

Yes, AI generators will be able to pump out novels for novices without them having much knowledge, because the AI will prompt them each step of the way, but if you don't understand writing craft, you will not know the language the AI uses when they ask you things like 'What character arc do you want for George' and other questions the AI may ask you in the process of creating the book. Without some knowledge and skill in writing, you will not be able to make educated decisions, direct the AI effectively or evaluate its responses. And during my research for this chapter, it became clear early on that some of the AI suggestions, even in ones designed specifically for writing, had major faults when I evaluated them according to the knowledge contained in this book.

How Much AI Usage Makes an AI Written Book?

Don't get me wrong here; I am not advocating *for* AI usage in the arts, but I am not against using it judiciously either. AI is here to stay. Many people reject it outright, and that's fine; but many, if not most of us, will probably eventually use it to some degree. We already use it every time we use a spellcheck or read the AI summaries in our internet searches. Those wanting to reject all AI writing and point their fingers at authors who use it, need to be aware of the difficulty of discerning at what point exactly you could say a book was 'AI written'.

For instance, what if you used AI to give content suggestions and create the outline for a chapter of a non-fiction book using information readily available on the web. You know enough about the topic to be able to evaluate the truth of the suggested content, but the AI can save you time in delineating and ordering the material. This is a very specific and limited usage. Does this make it an AI written book? What if it was three chapters out of twenty? Or ten? At what point do you say that the book is AI written? Especially if the AI didn't write the prose; it just helped with the structure. In this example, it seems clear to me that whether used for one or all chapters, the AI is used as a tool to assist the author, not as a replacement for the author. I would not say that such a book was 'written' by AI, but others may disagree.

What if you use it to lay out the structure for your novel, to short cut the process of outlining, and refining the outline, but you write the words yourself? Is that an AI written book? What if you get it to write the first draft as well and then rewrite it using the AI draft as you would dot points, just a reminder of what you want in that chapter? Is that an AI written book? If you have an AI do *all* the writing at *every* stage, then it's clearly AI written, but in most cases, I expect whether to call something AI written or not won't be so clear cut.

I don't doubt that plenty of readers won't care that a book is fully written by an AI as long as it's a good story. Others will care and will seek out human-written works—and if you've written all of it yourself, without any AI usage, then make that clear to readers. But as readers, we need to understand that AI-written books are not *created* by AI. They are created by a human being *using an AI tool* to assist in the process. That means that the author of an AI written work is responsible for both the deficiencies and the depth of insight in the text, just as they are for any book. When evaluating AI usage in writing, it's not just a matter of 'all AI usage is bad' or 'all AI usage is okay'; when AI *is* used, we must also ask *How well is it used?* Even in books fully written by AI, there will be both good and bad AI-written books. And which side of that determination a book falls on depends on the skills of the author, the person who directs the AI, not the AI itself.

Because AI can be used in various ways without having it write the whole book, the question of whether a book is written by AI often cannot be answered with a simple yes or no. But authors who do use it will need to use it judiciously, so they don't lose their sense of ownership of the writing or their sense of satisfaction in the process and the final product. And if the purpose of writing your book is therapeutic, or the therapeutic value you get from writing is important to you, then any AI usage is contrary to your aims, and clearly you need a human being with human sensitivities to edit the book if you choose to publish it.

AI has advantages and disadvantages, and I hope this chapter will alert you to these. I have experimented—with great discernment—with

ChatGPT and some specialised writing AIs to discover their capabilities and their limitations, so I could make an informed decision on AI usage for this chapter. You can also experiment or not. But when you come to evaluate what you get, bear in mind the following.

Author Voice and the Limitations of AI

With AI usage, you might end up with something that sounds good—at least at first glance—and saves you time, but you might feel little satisfaction—if any—if you haven't brought forth those words from your heart yourself. For instance, if you write because you love written language and have a passion in your bones for expressing yourself in words, or you write because it helps you make sense of the world, or you're developing a new theory about something, then AI usage will be in direct opposition to your aims.

Unless you ask for a specific style and voice, AI writing will always be somewhat generic. This is because they scrape their training data from everything openly available on the web, and their output style is a mix of it all. AI article writing, for instance, if you don't program the AI for a specific style and tone, has a kind of bland know-it-all voice that can use a lot of words to say what can be, when evaluated closely, actually very little. They essentially repeat what everyone else has said on a topic and seem to skim the surface, speaking in generalities. If you ask them to use a first-person voice and speak about the human experience of yoga, for instance, they will sound like every wellness blog ever written.

There's a lot of this kind of generic AI-written material being churned out for business blogs, and I can see how convenient it is for businesses to use AI in this way, but as authors, we can hopefully offer more than bland. In this environment, the only way to add something of value to a discourse is through personal human experience—your experience, not an AI's simulation of it.

As individual human beings, we each have our own way of speaking, thinking and writing. Yes, we use the same language as others, but within that, we have our own unique framework and way of seeing the world. When we write from that personal framework, we develop what's known as an author's voice. What brings a book from the realm of the ordinary into the realm of the extraordinary is the strength of the author's voice. Books written through strong voices are gifts to the world, gifts with the power to influence minds and change cultures. An author's voice is unique, and it usually takes considerable writing experience to develop your voice and know what it is.

'By its very nature, AI identifies and follows established patterns. Given the chance, it will flatten your voice until you sound more like everyone else and less like you, by "correcting" your creative language and forcing it to adhere to certain grammatical rules. No matter how you instruct it, AI will almost always fall back to doing this.' https:// indiereader.com/2025/07/do-you-really- need-a-proofreader-in-2025

If you consistently get an AI to write the words for you before you know what your voice is, you will never develop your own voice. The likelihood of you ending up becoming a generic writer with no voice of your own is high, and that's a terrible shame because your voice is what's important for you as an author and for your readers. And if you think the AI writes better than you do, watch out that you don't unknowingly start to copy the generic AI style. God forbid that we all end up sounding like bots!

Every word of your own that you write and publish is your contribution to our world, no matter how small, which is, I suspect, why my personal experience of using an AI to write a blog post was dissatisfaction. It left me feeling somewhat hollow. Despite asking for it to be written in my style, and giving it detailed instructions for what to include, it didn't sound or feel quite right—so much so that I ended up deleting the blog post. Only after a very detailed examination did I realise where it fell short.

AI, Authenticity and the Risk of Diminishing Ideas

You could use an AI to write your blog posts or stories and pass them off as your own—after all, the ideas are yours, right? Or are they? That depends on how well you've prompted the AI and how well you've evaluated and edited the results. Using AI well is a skill, and it's easy to use badly. You could ask an AI to write in the style of Hermann Hesse and get something extraordinarily beautiful and moving, but though it may be written in accordance with your ideas, it's not *your* style, not *your* words, not *your* voice.

You can, of course, ask an AI to write in your

own voice, but you can only do that with any confidence once you know what your voice is. It's more than your style; it's everything you care about and how you perceive the world. Your voice comes from the ineffable you that can't be fully quantified; an AI can analyse our voice, but it doesn't always fit neatly into a set of parameters. To get an AI to write in your voice, you will need several books under your belt already and a writing AI that can handle you uploading several of them for it to analyse. This is not advisable for a beginner. Only after I'd written six novels could I begin to recognise my voice. Had I used AI during that time, I wouldn't have found that voice.

If you—as an experienced and technically knowledgeable author—do train an AI to write in your voice, you need to be able to see if and where the AI is doing your ideas a disservice or diverging from your perspective. The trouble here is that the ability to perceive subtle distortions in language—of the kind that can be introduced by AI—is an advanced editing skill, so you could be not saying exactly what you want to say and not realise it. And it's not so easy to see what's missing from something you read. What you get from an AI will read well, but are you certain that your ideas are fully fleshed out? And is there enough of you in the finished product for you to feel satisfaction that you wrote it? Experienced authors with several books behind them will be much more likely to be able to make this kind of discernment than inexperienced authors.

After playing around with AI quite a bit in article writing, I have found it tends to both diminish and subtly distort my ideas. Originality and personal perspective are squeezed into the generic experiences that populate the web from the loudest or the majority of voices. The most extraordinary and unique aspects of something I've written as a prompt, or text I've provided as a basis of an article, can be simply left out. Unless I am careful to insist that something is included, anything that is outside the commonly accepted parameters of a topic tends to be ignored. That's the risk of having an AI do the writing for you.

If you use AI to give you dot points to cover on a subject, that can be very helpful, BUT can you see what it didn't include that, had you thought about it, you would have included? If you do use AI in this way, remember that an AI will not include your personal perspective on a topic unless you can tell it what that perspective is. Best is that you jot your own dot points down first and then ask the AI.

Using AI 'Just' for Research? Be Careful

Even if you think, 'I'll just use it for research', be very careful, because it's well known now that AI gets things wrong. The old-fashioned way of researching, going to the original articles and painstakingly checking the sources, is the only way to be sure of your research. What you can get with the general ChatGPT and search engine AIs is a quick summary, but it's unwise to rely on that for details, for instance, of a particular time and place. You have no idea where that information has come from. It could be from something fictional. AI doesn't know the difference between fiction and nonfiction. It just scrapes all its information for answers to the questions that you ask and gives you a synthesis of what it finds that it thinks will answer the question in the way that you want it answered. The likelihood of distortion of what you think are facts is incredibly high.

> *'At first glance, it [AI] sounds like a dream tool for knowledge workers. A closer look reveals significant limitations.*
> *Many early tests have exposed shortcomings:*
> • It lacks context. *AI can summarise, but it doesn't*

fully understand what's important.
- It ignores new developments. *It has missed major legal rulings and scientific updates.*
- It makes things up. *Like other AI models, it can confidently generate false information.*
- It can't tell fact from fiction. *'It doesn't distinguish authoritative sources from unreliable ones.'* [1]

Have you ever checked the links attached to an AI summary and found that the information in the summary is not actually in the article? Or in any of the articles. I have. Enough times to know not to use general LLM AI for research—not if you want facts. And how often does it reference Reddit threads for its answers? AI doesn't know the difference between opinions (which is what drives Reddit threads) and facts as determined through scientific methods or first-person accounts delivered through reputable unbiased sources.

'AI hallucination is a phenomenon where, in a LLM often a generative AI chatbot or computer vision tool, perceives patterns or objects that are non-existent or imperceptible to human observers, creating

1. https://www.sydney.edu.au/news-opinion/news/2025/02/12/openai-deep-research-agent-a-fallible-tool.html

outputs that are nonsensical or altogether inaccurate.' https://www.ibm.com/think/ topics/ai-hallucinations

Even using the Scholar ChatGPT tool, I found that the links provided didn't work—the site directed to couldn't be found—or they went to works that were not directly relevant to the question, and I couldn't see how the AI came to its 'this article shows that …' summary. It's important to remember that one cannot trust AI to get it right.

Another point when using AI for non-fiction writing is that it may not determine which facts are crucially important and which are minor, so if you get it to write a blog post or a chapter about a historical event or a famous person, it may fail to properly place enough weight or importance on the pivotal facts, unlike a human with a degree and/ or analysis skills. Someone using AI for research in this way may be misled even after verifying the information is accurate because information that is much more important is missing or understated.

Where AI Can Help

AI is excellent for writing promotional copy (something I'm particularly bad at myself), and it can be good for ideas when you get stuck, like brainstorming titles and character names. It works well for summaries and shortening or repurposing long articles (though check that it hasn't left out the most important points and that it hasn't taken away your voice). It can help turn a rough transcript of you talking into a blogpost or a blog post into a video script.

In article writing, I've found it's useful for the occasional paragraph, for instance, when I want a quick summary of the meaning of something relevant to the overall topic that I don't want to go into in too much detail. It can save me a lot of time trying to get something succinct enough. But even then, you need to check carefully, because AI tends to reinforce stereotypes and biases. Never ask it to summarise anything that you haven't previously researched, because if you don't already know the topic, you can't check for incorrect information or subtle bias.

I advise writers who wish to use AI to do so with a very discerning editorial eye and not to use it as a replacement for a human editor. Use it in addition, not as a replacement.

The Value of Human Editing

An AI can never give a human perspective. It can only ever simulate it. We write for other humans, not for bots, so we will always need another human's perspective to be sure that our work is meaningful for our intended audience and that it fulfills our vision.

As time goes by, I assume that more authors will try AI for copy editing their books, just to check grammar, punctuation and spelling. You may think that's okay—harmless, you think—but you'll have to give it precise instructions if you don't want it to correct bad grammar in dialogue, for instance, or get rid of all your snappy fragments. Have you noticed how your Word grammar check wants to add words into fragments so they are full sentences? And have you noticed how terribly formal that sentence sounds after that change if you accept it? How it no longer sounds like you. That's the sort of thing an AI will do as a matter of its basic programming. Anything outside of the 'rules' will be removed because the AI can't discern if it's appropriate to leave it in. And, of course, because you can't trust AI, you will need to go through it all and check. You might, for instance, find some odd changes when you've used a word in a non-standard way. The opportunity for AI to misinterpret what you're trying to communicate is particularly strong when it comes to metaphors and subtle ideas—especially new perspectives. A human editor can apply the rules in a more nuanced way that allows for a much greater range of language usage.

And if you want an AI to edit for effective communication and beautiful prose, as in line editing, you risk losing even more subtleties in the translation. The AI will be able to make your words read well, yes, but at the cost of you developing or deepening a personal style. And as I quoted from the *Indie Reader* article previously, 'No matter how you instruct it, AI will almost always fall back to' flattening the prose into something more generic. A good line editor would never do that, because they are concerned with amplifying the author's voice and are careful not to diminish it.

I would never give a chapter of this book to an AI to line edit, for example, because it would—probably even if I ask it not to—remove the conversational nature of the writing. It would likely make me sound like a know-it-all professor giving a lecture. It would undoubtedly make it tighter and more succinct, but I have kept this book in this loose conversational style for a reason. I want the reader to feel like they're listening to a real person—and not just any person, but me—talking.

It's hard to explain how I, as an editor, respond to all the subtle shades of meaning in a manuscript when I edit someone's work. But I am aware of my brain drawing from a multitude of different subtle aspects of language and structure to evaluate each edit. I tune into the author's voice and what they are trying to say, and I make my decisions in alignment with their voice and their vision as if I were the author. I feel the words and their impact on me as much as I analyse them.

AI is a machine. It cannot have a human experience—no sensation, no emotion, no pain, no hope, no fear, no empathy—and that will not change. That is the limitation of AI. It cannot truly evaluate the effects words have on a human reader because it isn't human. That is why authors will always need human editors.

Would you really trust an AI to edit your book?

Trust Your Voice

I encourage you to have confidence that your voice, your individual way of writing about how you perceive the world and what you consider important, is what's important in writing. If you want to get deep satisfaction from your writing, knowing that you've put your heart and soul into your book, then you'll want to craft every word yourself, because there is no replacement for that skill and no greater value. Just as AI art—though it has its place—will never replace handmade traditional art, I don't think AI writing will ever replace traditional writing in terms of its cultural value. When every word is the author's own, edited by a human who understands the nuances of the author's vision, it's special in a way that AI-assisted writing can never be. And if that's your approach, I encourage you to make it clear to your readers. Use it as a marketing tool—every word my own creation!

But if you do want to use AI to assist you in parts of the writing process, I don't think you should feel bad about it, nor should you be demonised for it. But as with any tool, you do need to make sure you use it well, not badly. As an AI artist, I know how much skill is required to get really good results. Yes, you can get some good images with little work, but to go beyond the generic, then you need more skills than just the ability to describe a picture and accept the first thing that comes up. It's the same with AI writing. To go beyond the generic, you need skills and knowledge of the writing craft, skills and knowledge that can only be honed through the traditional writing path of—yes—doing it all yourself. And you need to understand the limitations of AI, how to get the best out of it, why you should never trust it to make decisions for you, and be aware enough of how it's optimised for 'customer satisfaction' not to be seduced by it.

My aim in this chapter is to help you make an informed decision on AI usage in your own writing, but I have two pieces of advice I want to share. First is to never use an AI to write the prose for a novel or a memoir, not if you want your writing to be something with the potential to be deeply meaningful for your human readers—and for yourself. I think it's important that the author write the actual words themselves because the author's personal point of view and human experience is so important in fiction and memoir writing, and it simply can't be replaced by something written by an AI. For light fiction, an AI simulation is probably enough, but not if you want your book to have some depth or new insight to it.

Second, don't let the AI do your thinking for you. That is probably the worst potential outcome from AI usage. Writing a book is exercise for your brain and having an AI do it all for you is like taking a robot to the gym to do your exercises for you—your muscles will atrophy. Research indicates that *reading* books helps keep dementia at bay, imagine how much more that must apply for *writing* books. At the very least, even with small AI usages, always evaluate the responses it gives you to see what it has missed out, where it might be reinforcing harmful stereotypes, diminishing important points, making something up, drawing unsupported conclusions, or presenting opinion as fact. It's tempting in a fast-paced world to accept the initial results and move on, but thinking about the output is vitally important if we are to retain the very important human ability of being able to think.

What AI can never replicate is the inspired words that come while writing in a deep creative space. Elements you never considered while planning (and so wouldn't have directed the AI to include) appear and add depth, richness, and unpredictability. Use AI for your creative writing, and you're doing everyone a disservice, especially yourself.

PART FOUR:
REVISING

The Second Draft

When writing your first draft, you use your creative mind to get your ideas down and leave your critical mind out of it. It's the fun part where you immerse yourself in the world of your story, and it doesn't matter how terrible your writing is. At the second-draft stage, however, you need to engage your critical mind to evaluate what you've written and then revise it.

Though creativity is still important, of course, your critical mind is what flags the problems for your creative brain to solve. If you or someone else doesn't pick up the problems, they'll still be there in the finished work. Anyone can write a first draft, but not so many can revise and self-edit a novel to the point where it can be called a good book. That's your challenge.

I managed it simply by sticking at it. My Chinese birth year is the Year of the Goat, and my stubbornness in not giving up on my early books and keeping on educating myself in the craft of writing is what got me there in the end— two awards for *Lethal Inheritance* prove that I turned that dreadful first draft into a quality work of fiction.

If I can do it, so can you. And I'm here to help you all the way.

Take a Break

Don't show your first draft to anyone. A first draft is like creative vomit: it comes out in an inspired gush, and no one wants to look until it's cleaned up. Getting feedback on a first draft is likely to make you miserable. Why? Because, unless you're an experienced author, first drafts usually have a lot of aspects that need to be improved.

It's important to give yourself space between finishing the first draft and looking at it again, so I suggest that you don't look at your manuscript for at least six weeks. Longer is better, and during that time, read other books in the genre—good books and ones that sell well. That will give you something to which to compare your book when you return to it.

The Second-Draft Tasks

The key thing you're involved in at the second-draft stage is evaluation, and the more objective you can be, the better. Let go of your attachment to what you've written, and be prepared to throw it all away if that's what's needed. Taking a month or so off from your book will allow you to take a step back from your story so you can see it more clearly.

Your first task is to read it through and make notes. Don't try to change anything; just note what needs to be changed. It's important to not break the flow of your reading and try to see what you were trying to write so you can strengthen it. You also need to check the story elements and improve them.

This is where you use your knowledge of writing craft to evaluate what you've written. So what follows isn't just a list of things you need to check before writing your second draft; it's a revision of everything I've already talked about.

- **Take a step back from your story**: Don't look at your manuscript for at least three weeks and, in the meantime, read some quality books in the genre.
- **Evaluate what you've already written without attachment**: Be prepared to completely rewrite

the book if necessary.

- **Identify your story's themes and strengthen them**: What are your underlying themes? Make sure they're clear and that you follow them through to some conclusion. (More on this in the next chapter.)

- **Check the plot**: Do you have a clear protagonist with an aim and an antagonist with conflicting aims that makes it hard for the protagonist to achieve their goals? These elements are necessary to create the dramatic tension that keeps readers reading.

Michael Hauge's "Six Stage Plot Structure"

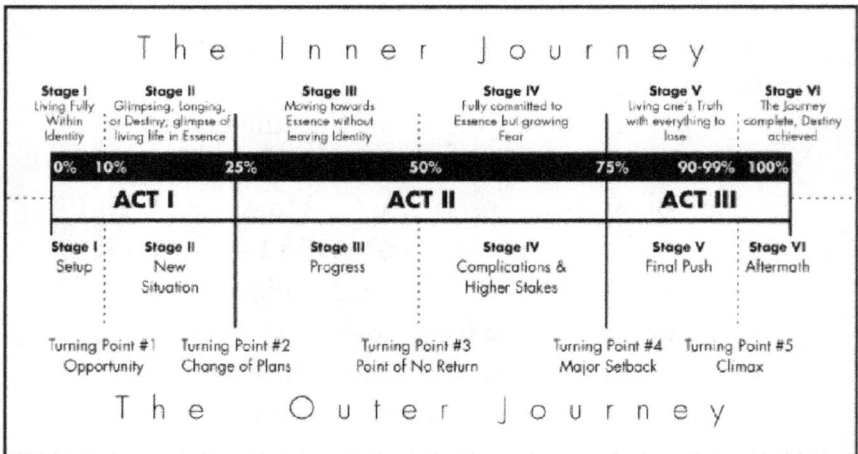

The	Inner	Journey			
Stage I Living Fully Within Identity	**Stage II** Glimpsing, Longing, or Destiny, glimpse of living life in Essence	**Stage III** Moving towards Essence without leaving Identity	**Stage IV** Fully committed to Essence but growing Fear	**Stage V** Living one's Truth with everything to lose	**Stage VI** The Journey complete, Destiny achieved
0% 10%	25%		50%	75% 90-99%	100%
ACT I		**ACT II**		**ACT III**	
Stage I Setup	**Stage II** New Situation	**Stage III** Progress	**Stage IV** Complications & Higher Stakes	**Stage V** Final Push	**Stage VI** Aftermath
Turning Point #1 Opportunity	Turning Point #2 Change of Plans	Turning Point #3 Point of No Return		Turning Point #4 Major Setback	Turning Point #5 Climax
The	Outer	Journey			

- **Do your plot points come at the right time to keep the reader interested?** Use a novel structure template such as *The Six Points of Story Structure* by Michael Hauge to help you plot the major changes, challenges and opportunities.

- **Do your characters have an inner journey as well as an outer journey?** How do the events of the story change your characters?
- **Scrutinise your characters' behaviour.** Make sure your characters act and react based on their previous experiences and knowledge and in accordance with their objectives.
- **Are there any scenes that don't move the story forward?** If there are any, cut them out. Every scene should have at least two reasons for being there.
- **Identify and evaluate subplots:** Do they have their own challenge for the characters involved? Do they add to your themes? Do they lead somewhere? The answer to these questions should be 'Yes'. If not, either add the needed elements or cut this aspect of your story back so it's not a subplot.
- **Does each scene have its own dramatic tension?** For example, a challenge the central character must overcome, an issue to be solved, an argument to finish, a task to complete and so on.
- **Does the pacing keep the story moving?** Are

there any points where the plot is lost behind big chunks of description, backstory or information? If so, break these elements into smaller pieces and spread them throughout the story.

- **Are your characters complex?** Do your characters have issues or emotional challenges or are they flawed in some way?
- **Is life too easy for your characters or too difficult?** Too easy is dull; too difficult is frustrating. Your characters need challenges. Things should not come easily for them, but they should have some successes.
- **Are your descriptions too detailed, too long or nonexistent?** Make sure you have some description, but not so much that it slows the pace.
- **Does the dialogue sound natural?** Is it how the characters actually would speak? Find out if it sounds right by reading it aloud. Make sure your characters don't all sound the same.
- **Is your worldbuilding clear and consistent?** Think your world through in detail. Be clear on the parameters, especially such things as magic and religious and cultural beliefs.
- **Is your point of view clear?** Are you writing in omniscient, intimate third person or first

person? Whatever it is, make sure that it is consistent throughout, and if you have changes in point of view, make sure that they are clearly flagged so you aren't head hopping or jumping from inside one character's head to another's.

- **Ensure that time flows consistently throughout your novel**. This entails verifying that the sequence of events and the pacing of your story are coherent and logical. Pay close attention to details such as the progression of days, weeks and months, as well as the timing of specific actions and dialogues. It's a good idea to make a timeline, and check that any mentions of days or months in the manuscript for events fall where they should on the timeline.

The Revision Process

After making notes in your manuscript of what comes to mind as you read with the above points in mind, it's time to do the rewrite.

A revision is not the same as a self-edit. At this stage we are still working with the big picture elements—plot, structure, character, dialogue, worldbuilding, etc.

- Delete any full chapters or scenes that you have

identified as unnecessary.

- If you have identified an issue with the plot or structure, then get any changes or additions needed on this point in place before working on anything else. This may require you to move scenes around. In that case, just move the chunk of text to its new place and don't worry about making it fit into the surrounding text at this stage. The idea is to get the new structure in place.

- After that, or if your plot and structure are strong or need only a little work, then you could start at the beginning and work your way through, or work on whichever chapters you are inspired to work on first, but however you approach it, read your story aloud as you go through it. This will alert you to any cumbersome sentences and unnatural dialogue.

The Emotional Challenge

Our emotional state can either help or hinder the writing process. I wanted the first draft of my first book to be perfect already, though I knew in my heart that it wasn't. I hoped I wouldn't have to do a lot of work on it, and that made it hard to see the faults. If you accept that your work is not perfect, you'll have no resistance to seeing the issues. If your book needs a lot of work, that doesn't mean you're a terrible writer; it just means you can improve it. And let's face it, we can all improve.

Be prepared to completely rewrite the book in the second draft if you consider it necessary. The more critical you are at this stage, the more time you will save yourself later. Probably my biggest mistake was that I resisted rewriting, but I had to do it in the end anyway. So don't resist the inevitable.

James A Michener emphasised how important rewriting is when he said, 'I'm not a very good writer, but I'm an excellent rewriter.'

You may have heard the saying, 'Kill your darlings.' This refers to the necessity of letting go parts of your story that you really like, that are possibly superbly written, but that don't move the story forward. Initially, I found that hard to do to the degree that was required, but eventually I realised that beautiful passages that don't add to the story actually detract from it.

So start your evaluation with the mindset that the book can be better, and you're going to find out how you can improve it.

Note that you need to do this initial revision before sending the book off to beta readers and editors.

Identifying and Deepening Themes in Fiction Writing

In his book *On Writing*, Stephen King mentions identifying your themes as part of the author's tasks at the second-draft stage of fiction writing. He says, 'I'm asking myself, What's it all about, Stevie ... what can I do to make those underlying concerns even clearer? What I want most is resonance, something that will linger a little while.'

I highly recommend this book to anyone writing novels. I read it early in my writing career and found it a big help. His analogy of writing a story as akin to an archaeologist uncovering bones rang true to me as far as my own process goes, so I always remember that as well as this advice on the importance of identifying and drawing out your themes.

Deep and Meaningful or Not?

Not all books are deep and meaningful. Sometimes we just want to read something light, but even so, even in the most frivolous book, there can be underlying themes that we aren't aware of when we write the first draft. If we identify them and draw them out when we do our second draft, we add another level of engagement to our work, a level that, as Stephen says, makes the book 'linger a little while' in the reader's mind.

We don't need to lay it on with a heavy hand—that's always counterproductive—it's just a matter of being aware of what we might be saying beneath our story and making sure that we give it enough definition so that the themes come through.

How to Find Your Themes

If you're not clear on your themes because you never set them before you began to write, that doesn't mean you don't have any. You may just not be aware of what they are, so look for them before thinking about adding anything in. Usually, the book's themes are already in what you've written in that first draft, and they only need to be found and strengthened. To find them, look at what you already have.

Ask yourself:

- What's the main point of the story?
- What am I trying to communicate to others through this story?
- Does the protagonist's struggle have significance for the reader's own life?

Deepening Your Themes

Your themes may not need deepening. It may be enough for you to identify them so you're aware of them during your revision process. Or you may simply not want to develop them further, and that's fine too. You may decide that developing them further is for a different book, that trying to develop them for this book may not be right for the story. All that is fine.

But you may find that by identifying the hidden themes, you gain new inspiration for the story, for events or characters' thought processes that acknowledge a theme or issue. It may raise possibilities for conflict between characters that can add more tension to otherwise lacklustre scenes, or provide a link between characters that can deepen their relationship.

For example, in a team situation, your female protagonist might not relate too well to the male engineer until she discovers that he feels as passionately about some issue as she does.

If you do gain further inspiration, that's great, but don't be concerned if you don't. It's just a worthwhile process in case there is something there you can develop further.

Can There Be Too Much Emphasis on a Theme?

The opposite of having no theme with which to deepen the story is for the theme to overpower the story. This is when a book gets preachy. And that's something to avoid, because no one wants to be preached at. If you write your book with the aim of delivering a message of some kind, then you need to be cautious that your writing doesn't fall on the wrong side of the line between examining a theme or issue and preaching.

We all have things that we're concerned about, and those concerns tend to naturally flow into our writing, either somewhere in the story or as a concern shared by a character, so even books that you don't intend to have a theme may have one locked inside. Your job is to find it and release it so you can develop it fully. Developing it fully, however, doesn't mean that it takes over the story. It's all a matter of balance.

How to Avoid Preaching

The key here is to examine an issue, not to state your views on an issue. You need to allow the reader to come to their own decision about whatever issue you raise, and you need to allow them to come to a different conclusion than the one that you personally take. If you're perfectly okay with a reader seeing things differently to you, then you'll be unlikely to preach. If you're determined to make everyone see the issue as you do, then your writing may be heavy-handed and come across as preaching.

Readers tend to discard preachy books in disgust.

How not to preach:

- Have characters with different points of view so that you present different sides of the issue.
- If you want your protagonist to be the messenger, then have them unsure of their position at the start of the book and provide

events in the book that lead them to a strong conviction by the end. The more complex the path they take to their decision, the less it will seem like preaching.

- Don't treat the subject in a black-and-white fashion. Issues are rarely that simple. Try to show all the shades of grey around the issue.
- Don't make the bad guy someone who is only bad because he or she takes the side of the issue you see as wrong.
- Don't dump information about the issue, either in dialogue or as part of the narrative. Tease it out in small pieces at the places in the story where it is natural that the reader might want some background.

Favourite Themes

When I was in dance theatre, a dance critic told me that choreographers tend to work with similar or related themes over and over, and that they just examine the themes in different ways. That may be the same for you, and even where it's understated, your concerns and interests as an author are part of what creates an author's voice. It's natural that we write about topics that concern us or that the topics that concern us bleed through into our stories, and we may or may not want to examine those topics in a major way. The degree to which you tease out a theme is entirely up to you and dependent on your reasons for writing the book and the kind of story it is.

The Art of Self-Editing

Self-editing is an essential skill for any writer, as it allows you to polish your work before sending it off to an editor. The more you can edit your own work, the less work your editor will need to do and, therefore, the cheaper your editing costs.

How is self-editing different to revising? When you revise a book, you're looking at the big-picture elements. When you're self-editing, you're looking at the writing in more detail. But as with the revision process, you will be relying on your knowledge of writing craft to guide you in assessing and improving your writing.

Refine Your Language and Style

See my book *The Elements of Active Prose: Writing Tips to Make Your Prose Shine* for more detail on the following points.

Use Adverbs and Adjectives Sparingly

Overusing adverbs and adjectives can weaken your prose and distract readers from the story's core message. Be selective when incorporating these descriptive elements, and use them only when necessary to enhance your narrative. Showing rather than telling in your writing will lessen the need for adjectives and adverbs, so always try to find another way to express your meaning before you rely on them.

Does Your Point-of-View Character Use Natural Language?

Your POV character's voice should reflect their unique personality, background and experiences. Whether they speak formally, casually or with a specific dialect, ensure their dialogue and narrative voice are consistent and genuine. This doesn't just apply to when they speak; it also applies to their narration if you're writing in first-person or third-person-intimate POV.

Strengthen Your Sentences

Eliminate Unnecessary Words and Phrases

During the self-editing process, identify and remove redundant words, such as qualifiers (e.g., 'a bit', 'a little', 'fairly') and circumlocutions. This practice will result in stronger, more concise sentences.

Write in the Positive and Avoid Redundancies

Emphasise what *is* happening in your story, rather than what isn't. Additionally, eliminate redundancies like '*past* history' and '*tall* skyscrapers' to further streamline your prose.

Enhance Your Descriptions

Be Specific and Evocative

When describing characters, settings and objects, aim for specificity and vividness. For example, instead of simply mentioning a dog, state its breed to create a clearer image in your reader's mind.

Utilise Similes and Metaphors

Similes and metaphors can add depth and creativity to your descriptions. However, ensure these comparisons stem organically from your POV character's perspective and experiences.

Engage the Five Senses

Incorporate all five senses (sight, sound, smell, taste and touch) into your descriptions to create a more immersive reading experience. This multi-sensory approach will enable your readers to fully engage with your story's world.

Provide Description Through Action

Whenever possible, convey descriptions through action and dialogue, rather than lengthy narrative passages. This approach will maintain your story's momentum and keep readers engaged.

Address Walk-on Characters and Autonomous Body Parts

Treat Walk-on Characters as Furniture

Walk-on characters should serve a specific purpose in your story without stealing the spotlight from your main characters. Treat these minor characters as 'furniture', providing just enough detail to establish their presence and role in the scene.

Eliminate Autonomous Body Parts

Avoid phrases that imply body parts are acting independently, such as 'His lips curved into a smile'. Instead, attribute the action to the character as a whole: 'He smiled.'

Eliminate Repetition and Mitigators

Don't Tell Your Reader Something Twice

Repeating information can frustrate and bore your readers. Ensure each sentence adds new information or builds upon previous details to maintain a dynamic and engaging narrative.

Remove Mitigators

Mitigators, such as 'appeared to' and 'seemed to', can dilute your prose and create ambiguity. Strive for clarity and decisiveness in your writing by eliminating these phrases.

Limit the Use of 'Was', 'Is' and 'Were'

Excessive use of 'was', 'is' and 'were' can make your prose passive and less dynamic. During the self-editing process, identify opportunities to replace these words with more active and engaging verbs.

Working With Beta Readers

Every author needs feedback from beta readers—people who read their book before it's published. It's far better to attend to problems in the story before sending it to publishers or self-publishing it, so we ask beta readers to let us know if they find any issues. Beta readers are not publishing professionals. They may be family or friends, but it's best if they're avid readers or author friends or members of a writing group. The beta-reading stage comes before sending the book off to an editor.

When you write a book, mostly you know what you're trying to say, but that doesn't mean that you've said it in your writing, or that you've said it in a way that someone else can understand. When you read it back, you know what it means because you wrote it, but you can never read it in the same way as someone who doesn't already know what it's saying. It's quite possible that what you've written doesn't come across to your readers the way you thought it would.

There is only one way to find out if you've said what you thought you said, and that's asking beta readers (and your editor in a manuscript appraisal) to read it for you and give you feedback. Because they've never read it before, they'll see things about it that you can't see because you're just too close to it.

You may think you know what your story is about, but if you haven't thought it through enough, the plot might hang together for you, but not for anyone else. Only another reader will be able to see the plot holes that have escaped your notice and can tell you that it doesn't quite work for a reader.

Sometimes you haven't developed a theme or character or scene strongly enough for it to come across to the reader in the way that you want it to. You see it a certain way in your mind, and you assume that the reader will see the same thing; only a reader can tell you that they don't see what you see.

Sometimes you've written some beautiful passages or chapters that don't move the story forward. They may say a lot about a character or their past, or be a lovely interaction, but they don't really have much to do with the actual story. All they do is slow the story down. You may have whole scenes that are beautiful but basically irrelevant. You probably won't see this because you love them so much, so you need someone else to point them out to you.

You need to know all these things before you finalise your book, and it's much easier for someone other than you to see them than it is for you to see them yourself. The point of having beta readers is to help you find any major issues you might have missed before sending it to an editor. Again, the more work you've done on your book before sending it to your editor, the cheaper your editing costs should be.

If you don't know anyone who could beta read for you, then just go onto editing. Your editor does everything a beta reader does but with more knowledge and experience in giving feedback. And if you're unsure of the feedback you get from one editor in a manuscript appraisal, get another editor's opinion as well. Having no beta readers and going straight to editing is better than having beta readers who have no real basis on which to give feedback other than that you know them and they're willing to have a read.

How to Get the Best Out of a Beta Reader

When you ask someone to read your work, I suggest that you take the attitude that their criticisms will help you to make your book better. Tell them not to spare your feelings and that it's best for you if they tell you exactly what they think, even if it's negative. Look forward to their criticism, understanding that the harsher they seem, the better your book will be when you've fixed the problems. It's better to have the criticism before it's published than afterwards when it's too late to fix it.

One critical beta reader is better than seven who pat you on the back and say, 'Well done', or who give vague feedback. The best beta readers are the most critical and the most specific in their criticism. They write notes on the manuscript as they go through, so you know exactly where the problems are. Beta readers are most effective when you give them guidelines for feedback. This is what I give to my beta readers:

- If you lose interest, please stop reading, and I'll send you a revised edition later. Tell me where I lost you and why.

- In general, does the story/plot work? Is there anywhere where it wanders or seems irrelevant to the central storyline?
- Does the story move fast enough? Tell me where you think it's too slow or too fast.
- Are there any scenes or sections that make you want to skip ahead?
- Is the beginning engaging? Does it make you want to read on? If not, why? Do you have any suggestions for improvement?
- Were any of the sections too slow? Were you bored? Where? Any idea why you felt this way?
- Did you like the characters? Why, why not? Were their motivations clear and their actions and dialogue realistic? Were the changes in point of view clear?
- What did you think of the ending? Was the story tied up satisfactorily?

Dealing with criticism isn't easy—though you get used to it—but there are ways to take the sting out of it, and I'll share some of those ways in the next chapter. In a nutshell, though, take your criticisms as the cloth that will make your gold shine, not the hammer that will smash it.

Potential Problems with Beta Readers' Feedback

Not every beta reader's feedback will be equally useful, so you need to evaluate the feedback you get in terms of how much the person knows about writing. All feedback is useful, but be careful not to pay too much attention to people without writing knowledge. The worst are those who think they know about writing but really don't. For example, someone whose knowledge of writing comes from primary school, where using fancy dialogue tags was considered preferable to 'said', might say that you've used too many 'said's and suggest that you use fancy tags like 'ruminated', 'opined', 'screeched' and so on. If you listen to them, you could go through and change the 'said's to fancy tags that your editor then changes back. In that instance, you probably did use too many 'said's, but—as you now know—there are more skilful ways to fix that issue than changing them all to fancy tags.

Another problem comes when you use friends and family who don't know anything about writing as your beta readers. They just want to be encouraging, so they tell you it's wonderful regardless of how they really feel. Even if you tell them not to spare your feelings, they don't want to jeopardise their relationship with you, so they won't tell you they don't like it, even if they hate it. You can come away thinking your book is great and get a big shock when an editor tells you all the issues.

I suggest leaving it until the review stage before you let friends and family read it. Once it's edited and really good, they'll be impressed.

Don't make changes to your manuscript that don't feel right to you just because someone has said you should. Listen to your gut. If something doesn't feel right for your story, it probably isn't. And if you're getting a lot of differing opinions on your book, so you don't know who to believe, then don't make any changes before you've had an editor take a look at it.

How to Evaluate Feedback on Your Book

Whether you get feedback from a beta reader or an editor who has completed a manuscript appraisal on your book, if the feedback is such that you're faced with a lot of work to rectify the issues or it seems unnecessarily negative, dealing with it can be difficult.

If you take negative feedback as personal criticism or a personal attack, defensiveness tends to kick in automatically, but it's easier to deal with criticism of your book if you understand the process of coming to terms with it. This is what tends to happen:

Shock: You thought your book was pretty good. You've worked so hard on it. It can't be true. They must be wrong.

Defensiveness: You criticise and reject

the reviewer/beta reader/editor and their evaluation. What credentials does the reviewer have anyway? What do they know? It's only an opinion. It doesn't mean anything. You tell yourself this to try to devalue the criticism. You want to be able to ignore it, so you try to prove that the person doesn't know what he or she is talking about. At this stage you won't see anything worthwhile about the person who gave the feedback, regardless of their qualifications.

Depression: You feel terrible, crushed, even devastated. If they are right (despite trying to dismiss the feedback, part of you says that at least some of it must be true), then you're a terrible writer, and you'll never be any good. (They didn't say that; it's what you're reading into it). You feel like giving up.

Letting go: You give up your defensiveness and seek a way out of your depression. You may give up completely for a time, or you forget the book and do something else. You may decide you're never going to write again, or that there are more important things in life, and you put your focus elsewhere. This isn't a bad thing. You need to let go in order to clear your mind so you can start fresh with renewed energy, and giving up is a way to let go, and so is putting your energy and focus elsewhere.

I recommend giving up for at least one minute. Totally letting go, even for an instant, is a very refreshing thing to do, and it realigns your priorities. The bare minimum here is letting go of your defensiveness. You have to come to a position where you're prepared to consider that perhaps the reviewer has a point and that, rather than rejecting it, you could learn from it.

Objective evaluation: After a break, you come back and look at the feedback in a more objective light. Okay, you think, what is this person actually saying here, and does it apply? If you don't let go, you can't do this. You'll remain stuck in defensiveness or depression.

Acceptance: You recognise the value of the feedback and see where it's valid. A professional view has more value than one from someone without professional experience in the publishing industry.

Moving on: You consider how to improve your work in light of the feedback, then do the work and improve the book. But if you just can't face working on it again, you put it aside and focus on improving your next book.

Satisfaction/gratitude: You recognise the improvement in the book, or at least in your knowledge, and are glad you went through this process.

Lessening the Pain

You can lessen the pain of dealing with criticism by cultivating a positive way of thinking. Watch the thoughts that come into your mind, and if you find your self-talk depressing, replace it with ideas that will have a positive impact. Consider telling yourself the following:

You are not your book. Criticism of your book is not criticism of you as a person, so don't take it personally.

It's feedback, not criticism.

Your integrity as an author is not diminished by one less-than-perfect book.

No book is perfect.

Most books can be improved.

Negative feedback will help you improve your work.

Let go of defensiveness so you can go directly to the objective evaluation stage.

Is the Feedback Valid?

Once you've got to the stage where you can put emotion aside and objectively evaluate the feedback, how do you do it?

Ask yourself the following:

- What education and experience does this person have in writing craft?
- Does the critic seem to understand my aims for the book?
- Does their criticism take into account the themes I'm working with? Would following their advice strengthen or diminish those themes?
- Are their suggestions in alignment with the kind of characters and story I'm trying to tell?
- Are they offering suggestions for the book they would write rather than supporting me in the book I'm trying to write?

Feedback from qualified people who have tuned into what you're trying to do, and whose suggestions will help you to achieve the kind of book you are trying to write, are the ones you want to pay attention to. If someone hasn't understood what you're trying to say or explore in your book, however, it means you haven't been clear enough.

PART FIVE:
EDITING

Why You Need an Editor

When I wrote my first book, I mistakenly thought that I could get a publisher without first employing an editor. I naively thought that they would see how wonderful my book was even in its raw state, and that they would hand it over to an editor to polish it up. That may have been the case back when authors wrote their books with pencil and eraser, and publishers had fewer submissions, lower overheads and less competition for sale, but these days publishers will discard any submission that isn't already well written. This is because no matter how brilliant the idea of your book, they don't want to have to spend a lot of money on editing it into something publishable. Also, they have so many submissions that only the very best will catch their eye.

Some self-publishing authors still have an unfortunate tendency to skip vital parts of the editing process, and it shows in their books. I'm not talking about a few copy errors; I'm talking about poor-quality writing in general, writing whose faults could have been eliminated simply by employing a professional editor.

Don't forget that no matter how much work you do on your book alone, you can never see what someone else will see in your work. Good feedback can save your book from disaster, and the best feedback will come from a professional editor.

The editor's role is to make your book better, and money spent on a professional is an important part of the writing process, not only to make sure your book is the best it can be but also because a good editor will teach you to be a better writer.

We Don't Know What We Don't Know

I got a manuscript appraisal for my first novel, and though it cost a lot of money at the time, it was a vital step in my writing journey because it showed me what I didn't know. We can't see what we don't know, so we need someone else to point it out so we can study it.

This makes it vital, especially for a beginner writer, to invest in their story and have a full comprehensive edit. I have seen self-published books that have been copy edited but not line edited, so there are no typos or grammatical errors—but the prose itself has significant flaws.

Had they worked with a line editor on their first book, they would have learned to eliminate these issues early on in their career. Instead, they have relegated themselves to the rank of a hack writer because they didn't invest in their career early on.

Copy editors don't improve the prose as a line editor does; they simply check the grammar, spelling and punctuation. Some also check for repetition and continuity, but they do not work on improving the author's ability to express themselves. A line editor can help you turn telling into showing, for instance, and will restructure cumbersome sentences.

Some authors mistakenly think that a line editor will change their writing too much, but this is a misunderstanding of the role of a line editor. A good line editor strengthens the author's voice and style; they don't diminish it. That said, I have heard horror stories of editors who overstepped the line and changed books into something the editor would have written, rather than improving the book the author had written. This is why it's important to get a sample edit for the line-editing stage, so you can see exactly what the editor will do to your work. It's not necessary to ask for this before a manuscript appraisal, however.

Look for an editor whose feedback from clients is that they improved the author's writing and taught them to be a better writer. My book on active prose has a section on choosing the right editor, so I won't repeat that here, but I will give a brief summary.

- Don't be seduced by the glossy websites and marketing spiels of big editing agencies. Those with the biggest marketing budgets aren't necessarily the best editors. The best editors are too busy editing to bother with marketing their services. Nor do they need to. They have a constant stream of books to edit from word of mouth alone.

- If you are considering a big agency, look into who will be editing your book. You might be better off with a freelancer where you can be sure your book won't be palmed off to the junior employee.

- Read the editor's blog posts to get a sense of the kind of person they are. Do they seem to understand an author's point of view?

- Check that they are experienced in the genre

of your book.

- Check out their qualifications, experience and author reviews.
- If you feel they might be a good match, then employ them for a manuscript appraisal. This is the first step of editing anyway, and even if you choose a different editor, professional opinions are always good to have. An appraisal should be relatively inexpensive, and you'll get a really good idea from their feedback if they are the right editor for you.
- If you don't want an appraisal, then ask for a sample edit and quote. These should be free, but they will not cover many words. Having an appraisal will allow you to get the full measure of an editor.
- Another option is to get a partial appraisal of the first couple of chapters.
- Once you have decided on your editor, it's very important that you trust them fully. If you don't feel you can trust their judgement, then it's better for both of you that you go elsewhere.

The Four Kinds of Editing

You may know that your book needs editing before publishing—I certainly hope so—but do you know the answer to the question, 'What does book editing involve?' You may not know what having your book edited actually means. I've seen books whose authors swear they've been edited, but all that's been done is a proofread!

A Proofread Is Not an Edit

Having your book edited isn't just finding someone to check that there aren't mistakes in grammar and punctuation. The story, characterisation, dialogue, worldbuilding and so on must be checked as well to make sure there are no plot holes and continuity problems. And (unless you're an experienced author who writes excellent prose) the prose needs to be worked on to ensure that it reads well—to make sure your book doesn't look like something a child might write.

Authors become too close to their work to see it clearly, and they can never see it from the perspective of a reader who has never read it before. But an editor can. It's like the difference between an aerial view and the view from a point on the ground. Authors need the editor's aerial view if they're to make their book the best it can be.

A full edit comprises all four forms of editing undertaken in the following order. Some books will need less work at different stages, and most books can have the line and copy edit done together, but all four areas need to be covered before you can say that your book has been fully edited and you can be confident that your book is a quality product.

The Developmental Edit

The developmental edit looks at the big picture: plot, pacing, characterisation, dialogue, structure and so on. Specifically, an editor will look at the book and ask:

- Does it have a strong plot and structure?
- Are the characters believable, well fleshed out and easy to relate to?
- Is the pacing too slow or too fast?

- Is there conflict and tension?
- Is the voice consistent?
- Is the point of view consistent, and are changes handled smoothly?
- Are there any unnecessary scenes, backstory or information dumps?
- Is it conceptually consistent in worldbuilding and themes?
- How can the author make it better at the structural level?

The editor will give specific suggestions as to how you can improve your work, usually in the form of a manuscript appraisal, after which you do a revision with their suggestions in mind. For the editor to make the changes themselves would cost a lot of money.

The Line Edit

The line edit:
- cuts unnecessary words and repetition
- turns passive prose into active prose
- checks word, metaphor and simile usage
- restructures sentences where needed for clarity, variety, rhythm and flow
- makes sure that your words make sense and

that you are saying what you want to say
- picks up inconsistencies in timing, descriptions, character actions and reactions and so on
- makes your prose read well

For beginning authors, a line edit makes the difference between a book that's professionally written and one that's not. Once you've worked with a line editor and learned from them, your editing costs should decrease for future books as your prose improves. This level of editing is often missed out by authors who are unaware of the difference between a line and a copy edit, and not every editor has line-editing skills. Some people, even some editors, think that a line edit is the same as a copy edit, but this is not the case.

Line editing is a special skill, more an art than the technical skill required for copy editing. A line editor not only knows everything a copy editor does, they also have a sense for the difference between pedestrian prose and exceptional prose and know how to improve prose while remaining true to the author's voice. Copy editors are much more numerous than line editors, and if you're not clear that you want a line edit as well as a copy edit, you may only get a copy edit.

Line editors are also copy editors and usually

do a copy edit at the same time, but in cases where a manuscript needs a lot of work at the line-editing level, they may do two passes of a manuscript, one focusing on the line edit, followed by one focusing on the copy edit.

The Copy Edit

A copy edit primarily corrects grammar, spelling and punctuation. This is the purely technical level of editing. A copy editor will not delete unnecessary words or suggest rewording where the meaning is unclear, nor will they restructure your sentences unless they are grammatically incorrect. Therefore, your book could be just as badly written after their edit as it was before, but it will have no grammatical, spelling or punctuation errors.

Once you have worked with a line editor on a couple of books, a copy edit will likely be all your subsequent books need. But it's still advisable to work with an editor who can also line edit so they can pick up any cumbersome sentences or areas where you could express your meaning with more clarity or precision. It's rare not to find a few places in a book where the prose could be improved, and you want an editor who will at least be able to point those places out to you. Generally, editors who can line edit are the more experienced editors or they are also authors.

An editor should also provide your manuscript with basic formatting, such that the manuscript is easy for agents and publishers to read, and easy for book designers to work with. If you haven't already set heading styles so they show up in the navigation pane in Word, for instance, then the editor should do this. Asking a prospective editor if they do basic formatting is a good way to weed out those who may not be as skilled as they might like you to believe.

The Proofread

Proofreading is done after formatting, whether it's formatting done in Word or the full ready-to-print PDF. The proofreader picks up typos, checks formatting and corrects anything the copy edit missed or errors introduced during formatting. A proofread is most effective when done by a different person, as it's unrealistic to expect a single editor to catch every error. Two sets of eyes are better than one if you want to avoid copy errors in your book—and don't we all? That said, don't expect not to find one or two. Copy errors have a way of slipping past even the best of us.

Now that you know the terminology and can answer the question, 'What does book editing involve?' you'll be able to better communicate with prospective editors. Be careful, though; if a prospective editor doesn't seem to understand the difference between a line and a copy edit, or their edit doesn't include basic formatting, I suggest you look elsewhere.

How to Review Edits

I wrote what follows for my own editing clients. Though other editors may—and likely do—work differently, much of the advice in this chapter applies in a broader sense. The reviewing tools I refer to here, for instance, are likely used to some extent by all editors and are certainly worthwhile knowing about.

Comments

A manuscript appraisal will have comments left on the manuscript. If you don't see any comments, go to the Review menu and click Show Comments. If you can't click on Show Comments, make sure Track Changes is set to show Simple Markup or All Markup. The Previous and Next buttons will take you to the previous or the next comment to save you having to scroll through the document to find them. The arrow in the Show Comments box allows you to choose Contextual or List to display them. I recommend the Contextual setting.

I leave comments for three reasons:

- To educate you by explaining why I have done something. These do not require a response from you.
- To indicate where there is an issue you need to resolve or something I need you to check. Comments in this category will also be bookmarked, so you can find them easily.
- A question means something is not clear in the text, and you will need to rewrite to clarify that.

Bookmarks

My editing process involves leaving bookmarks so you can find places in the document where I've asked you to check or add something or there is some issue to resolve. Bookmarks are not the same as comments. Bookmarks save you from looking through the document to find the comments I want you to look at. It's quite simple; just go to the Insert menu and click on Bookmarks. A box comes up, then you select the bookmark and click on the Go To button.

Word 365

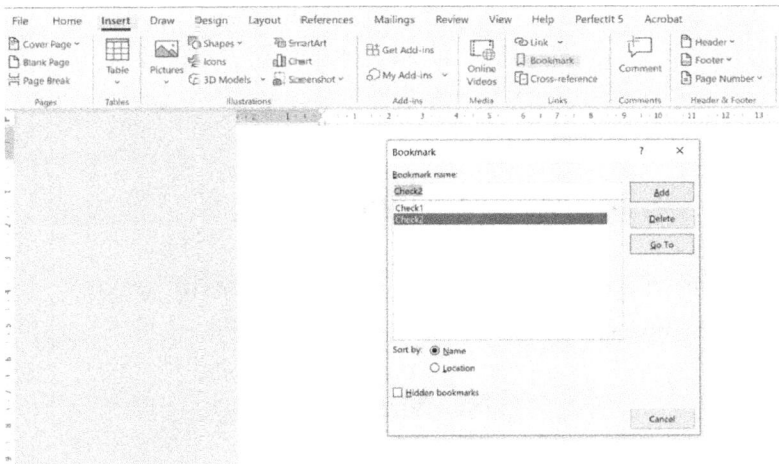

Adding a bookmark:

If you change something after the edit that I need to check, then you'll need to leave a bookmark so I can find it easily.

Just put your cursor in the spot you need to bookmark. Click on Bookmark in the Insert menu, as above, give your bookmark a name (recheck1, recheck2 etc), then click Add.

Track Changes

Track changes controls can be found on the Review menu. You can set how you want to view the document by choosing Simple Markup, All Markup, No Markup or Original.

Original

Shows you the original document without any changes.

No Markup

When set to No Markup, you will be able to read the finished manuscript without it showing what I deleted and what I added.

This is the easiest and least confusing way to check your manuscript. You can read it through without clutter, stop only if you find something you don't like, and then use the other controls to see what I did there. Once you've reviewed the edit, you then decide whether you want to accept it, reject it or rewrite it (see below).

Working this way allows you to see how the edited version sounds as you read. You'll be able to enjoy the writing as a finished product. If you try to see what was there before and how I've changed it (the markups) without reading the unmarked-up manuscript first, you will get bogged down in unnecessarily checking thousands of individual edits without ever getting a sense of the flow and rhythm of the edited prose.

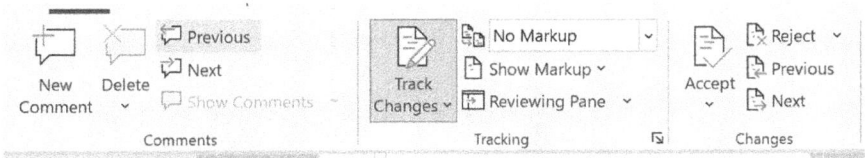

New Comment	Delete	Previous / Next / Show Comments	Track Changes	No Markup / Show Markup / Reviewing Pane	Accept	Reject / Previous / Next
Comments			Tracking		Changes	

Simple Markup

When set to Simple Markup, you'll see a red line on the side indicating that something has been changed. Where I have had to reformat the book into styles for easy formatting into an ebook and paperback (which is mostly the case), you'll find these red lines all the way through the document. Other than that, you can read the manuscript without the clutter of seeing all the edits and work with it in the same way as you would with No Markup.

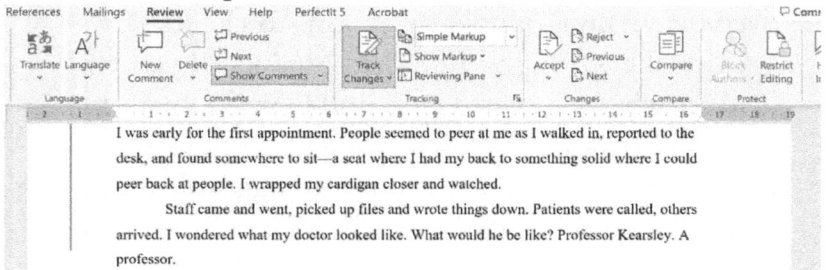

I was early for the first appointment. People seemed to peer at me as I walked in, reported to the desk, and found somewhere to sit—a seat where I had my back to something solid where I could peer back at people. I wrapped my cardigan closer and watched.

Staff came and went, picked up files and wrote things down. Patients were called, others arrived. I wondered what my doctor looked like. What would he be like? Professor Kearsley. A professor.

All Markup

Set Track Changes to All Markup when you've got to a point where you want to see exactly what I've done. This will show you both what was there (your original document) and what is there now. Deletions have a strikethrough. Additions don't.

I recommend only turning on All Markup when you find something in the manuscript that doesn't feel right to you. Then you can see what was there and how I changed it and decide if you want to revert to the original (reject the edit), accept it or rewrite it.

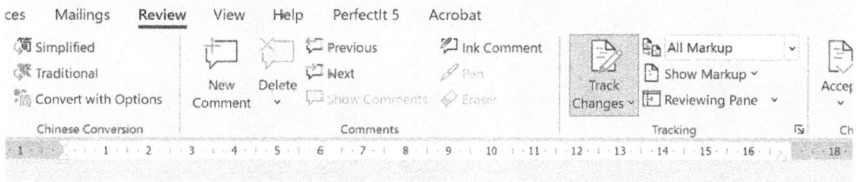

Chapter 2

Old Ham's Scare

You can choose to show the markups inline, as in the picture above (which can be confusing) or in balloons, as in the picture below. This version shows the additions in red and the deletions in the balloons on the side.

Select Balloons in the Show Markup drop-down options (the middle option in the Track Changes box on the toolbar), then choose either Show Revisions in Balloons or Show All Revisions Inline.

cried like my world was ending. My father came running in asking what she'd done to me. My first rebellion.

My second rebellion was over my hair. Mum always kept my hair short. Straight and short with a fringe. She called me a china doll. I was thirteen and my hair was getting a bit longer; the ends were dried and split. Mum wanted to get my hair cut short again. I said no.

'But it looks so messy, like rats' tails.'

'I want my hair to grow long.'

'But it looks so nice short; it's so easy to keep.'

'No, Mum, I want my hair long!'

So I got my hair trimmed only, and I grew it long for the rest of high school. My best friend envied it—'It's so shiny, so straight and neat.' And it was so long. I would put clips in the front or put it in a ponytail, or braid it, the heavy plait falling down my back. And released from the braid, it would fall in full, gentle waves. Other girls would say, 'My hair won't grow that long; it just falls out.' My hair made me feel special.

During a science class we were experimenting with static electricity. A student would stand on a plastic container and was 'charged up'. All your hair would stand out on end—the charge causing the hairs to repel each other. The class wanted me to have a turn. They charged me up. My long hair stood out, a huge wave of hair floating around my head. Everyone oohed and aahed. The teacher from the class next door happened to walk past, stopped to look, went back into his class and returned with his students—'Have a look at this!' My hair caused a

Tahlia Newland
Deleted:

Tahlia Newland
Deleted: ¶

Tahlia Newland
Deleted: "...But it looks so messy, like rats' tails."...

Tahlia Newland
Deleted: "...I want my hair to grow long."

Tahlia Newland
Deleted: ; "...b...ut it looks so nice short,... it's so easy to keep."....

Tahlia Newland
Deleted: "...No, Mu...m. - ... want my hair long!"....

Tahlia Newland
Deleted: ¶

Tahlia Newland
Deleted: ¶

The Show Markup drop-down options also allow you to choose to remove the formatting markup. Click Formatting to remove or add the check mark. No checkmark means the formatting changes won't show up. This allows you to focus on the textual changes—additions and deletions.

Accepting and Rejecting edits

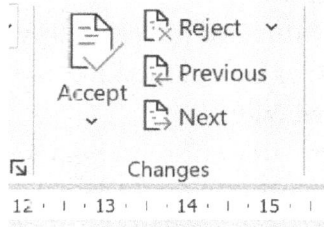

To the right of the view markups option, there is the option to accept or reject each edit. Click on the edit in All Markup view, and then click accept (to keep the edit) or reject (to return to the original). The Previous and Next buttons will take you to the next edit. You can accept or reject the change and stay where you are, or accept or reject and move to the next edit.

There are two kinds of edits:

- **Objective—the copy edit.** These are edits to correct grammar, punctuation and spelling/word use. *Don't reject these.* They are consistent with whatever conventions we're following—US (Chicago Manual of Style) or UK style.
- **Subjective—the line edit.** These edits are ones where good line editors will recognise there's a problem, but they may solve the problem in different ways. *Even if you don't like my*

solution and reject the edit, the original still has a problem that you need to solve. Line edits are such things as:

- deletions due to overwriting, repetition, diversions, or lack of forward movement in the scene or overall plot
- shifting the order of sentences and paragraphs to keep a logical flow of ideas
- restructuring or rewriting sentences for better prose, clearer communication or consistency with the way a character would talk

The arrow below Accept gives you the option to Accept All, so once you've checked a few edits, if you're pretty sure you'll like everything else, you don't have to go through them all individually.

Often, I alter something because the original is clunky or not clearly expressed, but my suggestion may not be something you like, in which case, rather than return to the original, it's best to write an alternative to my fix. That way, the result of the process will still be better than the original. In this case, you'll need to either accept or reject my edit and then change what you want.

When you go through, if there's anything you've changed that you want me to check for copy errors, leave a comment, bookmark it and send it back to me.

When you're happy with the manuscript, Accept All edits to clean up the document ready for proofreading. You can delete all comments by clicking the arrow on the Delete Comments button.

PART SIX:
PUBLISHING

Publishing Options

Publishing options today are many and varied, and unfortunately, it's an area rife with people more interested in taking your money than helping you produce a great book. Those who tell you things that sound too good to be true (like your book is the best thing they've read in years, it's going to be a bestseller and their $7,000 promotional package will ensure this) may be outright scams. I've seen adverts on Facebook and Instagram that promise authors can make tens of thousands of dollars publishing books on Amazon after just three months of writing (with their help, of course). One even promised that kind of income from books with no writing involved! These kinds of claims are blatantly untrue. The truth is that no matter how you publish your book, most books don't sell many copies. Very few authors make sufficient money from their books to be able to leave their day job.

Between 500,000 and 1,000,000 [2] *new books are published in the US each year, and the median book sells around 200 copies per year and less than 1,000 over its lifetime. Data from 2020* [3] *revealed that only 268 titles sold more than 100,000 copies, and 96 percent of books sold less than 1,000 copies. Just 2% of books* [4] *sold more than 5,000 copies.*[5]

Legacy Publishing

Mainstream or legacy publishing is selective. It requires you to submit your manuscript to literary agents and publishers, then they pay the costs of publishing and give you royalties from the sales. It doesn't cost you anything to publish this way, not even for any further editing your book might

2. https://www.tonerbuzz.com/blog/how-many-books-are-published-each-year/

3. https://www.elysian.press/p/creator-economy-for-fiction-authors

4. https://www.nytimes.com/2021/04/18/books/book-sales-publishing-pandemic-coronavirus.html

5. https://ryanlanz.com/2024/01/31/who-else-wants-to-know-how-many-copies-novels-actually-sell/

require after you've signed the publisher's contract. But the process takes a long time, and very few books are selected. It's usually several months before you hear back from a major legacy publisher, and mostly your manuscript will be rejected. They look for books that will sell well and that are skilfully written so they don't have to spend a lot of money on editing, so if your book has already had developmental and line editing, they're more likely to read it all the way through.

But if your book is unusual or only for a niche market, you'll not score a deal, because sales are most important for legacy publishers. After all, they put up the money for publishing, so they want books that will make that money back for them.

If you do get a deal, it is usually another eighteen months before your book will hit the shelves, and then ... well, let's just say, it's a highly competitive field.

I got an agent for my first book, *Lethal Inheritance*, but missed out on several publishing deals because they 'had enough young-adult books for the year' or they already had a couple of books with demons in them lined up for publication. The editors at one publisher loved the book, but the marketing department didn't know how to sell it. The marketing department has the final say.

Self-publishing Service Providers and Vanity Publishers

These are companies that will publish anyone's book regardless of its quality, but the author pays. With these services, you're self-publishing without doing it all yourself. It's still self-publishing because you are the one who decides if the book is worthy of publishing, not a publisher. Here, you give them your book, and they publish it for you, but with these services, you should also have the final say over the cover and amount of editing undertaken. Because they publish virtually anything submitted to them and generally do limited editing, the quality of books produced by such companies may not be particularly good. If you publish with a company that publishes inferior books, you place your book in the same category.

Vanity presses are self-publishing service providers who pretend to be legacy publishers. Their websites aren't upfront about the fact that the author pays, and they may say they have a submission process, but still publish anything that comes their way. Their prices and promises are inflated, so what you really get is few sales and an empty pocket. They prey on authors who don't have the knowledge I'm providing now. Hints that a publisher may be a vanity press include such things as:

- copy and paste responses to your emails
- appealing to your vanity in their initial communications
- low author royalties despite the author paying for publication
- sales promises
- highly priced promotional packages
- pressure tactics in trying to get you to sign a 'deal'
- set prices for editing (books have differing editing needs)
- running limited-time sales with big savings (if they can do this, their normal price is overpriced)
- a lack of authors publishing several books with them
- they are run by people without literary experience of any kind
- their books tend to be poorly written and edited
- their covers are generic

I have seen books published by vanity presses where the author has paid for 'editing', and yet the book is full of basic flaws, such as major plot issues or copy errors. Unfortunately, the authors only discovered this after getting poor reviews. Several such authors came to me after this experience and asked me to re-edit and republish their books.

If you take the self-publishing service route, you need to have had the editing done yourself beforehand, because you cannot trust most of them to do it for you, even if you pay for 'editing'. What they call 'editing' could just be a proofread. But most books need all four kinds of editing. It may seem like you're saving money by not paying for a comprehensive edit, but a poor product, even one with a high promotional budget, won't sell well in the long run, despite what scammers will tell you.

There are a lot of different companies in this category, but the ones known as vanity publishers will still, even after you've paid for the publishing, take a large chunk of the income from sales— sometimes giving authors as little as 30%–50% of royalties. This never seemed fair to me. If you're paying for publishing, you should be getting most of the income from sales—80% or more.

Hybrid Publishers

A hybrid publisher operates as a legacy publisher in terms of its standards and book selection process, but the author funds the publication. They have a genuine selection process, as with legacy publishing, and will reject books that aren't of a high-enough standard to compete with mainstream published books. They may, however, (as Alkira Publishing does) offer to work with the author to improve their book if they see potential in it. In hybrid publishing, the author should get the majority of the income from sales.

This kind of publisher is a growing breed, and my publishing company, Alkira Publishing, is one of them. Hybrid publishers do not all operate the same way, so you need to examine your options carefully. Some vanity publishers call themselves hybrid publishers to get away from the stigma of the term 'vanity publisher', so check for all the signs listed above and read one of their books to check the quality.

The beauty of hybrid publishing is that because the author funds the project, the publisher does not have to take potential sales into account when selecting from submissions. This means that if your book is unusual, groundbreaking or for a niche market, you'll still have a good chance of it being selected. And if your book is selected, then you get a stamp of approval similar to getting a legacy publishing deal. Your book is not self-published and so avoids that stigma. It is author-funded, but it has been selected because the publisher believes it's worth publishing; they're not publishing it just because they're being paid to do so.

Requirements for selection vary from company to company, but in the case of Alkira Publishing, since it's an offshoot of my editing business, I don't need to publish lots of books to make an income, so I can afford to be highly selective.

The quality of books published by hybrid publishers also varies from company to company. Because they have a selection process, they should be more likely to produce a quality product than a self-publishing service provider, but it all depends on the people making the decisions and on what kind of editing they do or require the book to have had before selection. Either way, you'll be paying for publishing.

Self-publishing

True self-publishing is doing the publishing yourself. It's the cheapest option, but also the most time consuming, because you have to learn a whole new business. And the quality of your product depends on how well you learn your business and the quality of the professionals you employ to help you. The wealth of information you need to know and the decisions you need to take can be overwhelming, which is why many authors are happy to pay someone else to do the publishing for them.

If you want a quality product (and why wouldn't you?) then even if you're self-publishing, you can't avoid paying professionals to do your cover, editing and ebook formatting. The likelihood of making embarrassing mistakes is great for first-time self-publishers. I had been warned, and yet I still made them when self-publishing my first books.

You can format the paperback interior yourself quite simply using Word, but you'll probably make mistakes that, to anyone who knows about book formatting, will scream 'self-published'. Getting your margins and page numbering right isn't easy the first time around, and did you know that the first line of any chapter or section break is not indented? Also, you must prepare the document to meet the printer specifications. For Ingram Spark, you'll need professional Adobe Acrobat software to do that. There's a lot to learn, and it's very time consuming and easy to make mistakes. So paying a professional to do it for you is worth it to avoid the headache.

Once you have your files, you can easily upload them yourself to Amazon for both the ebook and paperback, and that's fine if you live in the USA or the UK and only want to sell your book in those countries. (Amazon will sell them elsewhere, but they take most of the money). If you're in Australia or New Zealand, however, and you take this option, you'll have to buy your book from Amazon's printers in the US and pay international postage. Getting a box of books to sell yourself is not practical.

If you want international distribution so readers can order your book through any bookshop, you'll need to go through Ingram Spark. They have a printer (Lightning Source) in Australia, making it easy for Australians to get their book at a decent price.

Doing it Cheap or Doing it Well

Some people skip editing, do their own cover and even their own ebook formatting. There's free software for creating ebooks, and some ebook platforms allow you to upload a Word document that they then turn into an ebook, but you'll not get the best results that way.

And ... You probably think that the cover you designed looks good, but a graphic designer will be rolling their eyes in horror, and readers will skip your book because it doesn't look professional. Do you trust yourself to know what you're doing enough to risk using a cover you've made yourself?

As for editing ...

Remember that there are four kinds of editing, and for a book to be fully professional, it needs all four kinds: developmental editing, line editing, copy editing and proofreading. And though your family members and friends can give you feedback on your story, only a publishing professional will give you the kind of detailed guidance you need to be sure that you're not producing a lemon.

If you want your friends and work colleagues to be impressed with your book instead of embarrassed for you, you're going to have to fork out some money even if you are self-publishing.

Which Publishing Option is Best for You?

You've written a book—or you're in the process of writing one—and now you're wondering: '*How do I publish this thing?*' Do you go the traditional route, submit to publishers and hope for a contract? Or do you take matters into your own hands and self-publish?

This chapter looks at the pros and cons of each publishing model: traditional publishing, self-publishing and hybrid options. But the truth is, there's no one-size-fits-all answer. The right choice depends on your goals, budget, timeline and how much control you want over the process. Start with the big question: 'What Are Your Publishing Goals?'

You might assume that the aim of any author

in publishing their book is to sell lots of copies and make money, but that is not the only aim. In fact, many authors consider that to be a bonus if it happens because meeting their aims doesn't depend on selling a lot of books.

Why Are You Publishing Your Book?

Here are a few common reasons:
- You want to build a career as an author.
- You want a beautiful book to give to family and friends.
- You want to share your story or ideas with the world.
- You want a book to support your business.
- You want to record an event.
- You simply love the idea of seeing your name on a professionally produced book.

Each of these goals can lead you to a different publishing path. And that's okay. The important thing is that your choice reflects *your* aims—not someone else's expectations.

All of these aims do not require large sales for the book to be successful in terms of their aims. The publishing industry tends to operate as if making big sales is the objective of all authors. Certainly, we would all like that, but the reality is that few books become bestsellers. Having a goal that can be met without large sales is a surer way to feel some success.

But how does your aim (or aims) affect which publishing method you choose to pursue? Quality of the final product is a major determinant of one's choice of publishing method as it steers you away from vanity presses and self-publishing services in favour of hybrid publishers or mainstream publishers.

If the book is primarily for family and friends, then choosing a publisher with a marketing component will be a waste of money. If the book is to complement talks or an established business, however, you must choose a publisher flexible enough to incorporate business branding elements into the book's design.

Understanding your aim for the book will help you determine how many people might be interested in it, and the answer to that question will affect whether you publish or not. If your book is simply recording an event, for instance, consider how many people will be interested in that record? Could your purpose be fulfilled by having a few spiral-bound copies printed by a local printer?

Self-Publishing: Pros & Cons

Self-publishing gives you full control. You choose your service providers, and you get to keep the majority of the profits. It's fast, flexible, and can be incredibly rewarding—especially if you're entrepreneurial or enjoy learning new skills.

But it also requires:

- a willingness to invest in professional editing and design
- time to learn the publishing process or the budget to pay for support
- ongoing responsibility for marketing and distribution

Traditional Publishing: Pros & Cons

Traditional publishing is validating, and it opens doors in the industry, but it also means:

- long wait times (often years)
- little or no control over your book's design, pricing and timeline
- lower royalties compared to self-publishing
- your manuscript may not be accepted
- It's an excellent option if you're aiming for literary awards, wide distribution, or career-

building through a traditional platform—but it's not the only way to be successful.

Hybrid Publishing

Hybrid publishing falls between self and traditional publishing—the author pays to publish, but the publisher curates the titles through a selective submission process. Of course, your manuscript might not be accepted by hybrid publishers either, but they are more flexible on what they can publish than mainstream publishers. They are also more willing to work with the author to bring their book up to standard.

This model can work well if:

- You want your book to have the kudos of being chosen by a selective publisher, but you want to retain rights and a high degree of creative control.
- You don't want to jump through the hoops involved in chasing mainstream deals.
- You like the high royalties of self-publishing but don't want to learn the business or manage the process alone.
- You have a decent budget and high standards.
- You want a strong editorial team to help you polish your book.

- You're looking to learn the ropes of publishing as you go.

Self-publishing Services

The advantage of a self-publishing service over a hybrid publisher is more control. Your book doesn't have to meet anyone else's standards but your own. This is the best option for family histories, books to support businesses, those with a limited editing budget and works that push the boundaries of modern literary expectations.

The downsides of non-selective author-funded publishers are that there are no quality guarantees and little editorial assistance.

Choosing Based on Who You Are

What you choose from the available publishing options also depends on the following factors:
- **Your goals**—Is this a career move, a passion project or a business tool?
- **Your budget**—Can you afford to hire professionals if you go indie?
- **Your time**—Do you have time to query, wait or learn the ropes?
- **Your skills**—Are you comfortable with tech

and project management?

- **Interest**—Are you interested in learning the publishing business?
- **Quality**—How important is quality for you?
- There's no right answer that works for everyone. And you don't have to stick with one model forever. Many authors begin traditionally and later self-publish, or vice versa.

Publishing a book is exciting—but it's also a big decision. If you take the time to reflect on your goals, do your research and invest in quality where it matters most (editing and design!), you'll make the right choice for *you*.

You don't have to follow someone else's path. You just need to know where you want yours to go.

Examples

If you are relatively young and want a career in writing, then I advise you to invest in a comprehensive edit of your first book to make sure it's excellent, then try the mainstream route. If that doesn't work out, and you're tech and business savvy and interested in learning about publishing, then go straight to self-publishing. Learn thoroughly and do as much of it as you can yourself, but make sure you employ a professional cover designer. You will already have had your book fully edited, so spending on a cover design and setting some money aside for book promotion and your book launch is all you'll now need.

If you have little time or interest in learning the publishing industry and the legacy publishing route doesn't work out, go for a hybrid publisher with a genuine selection process. This way you'll get a quality product, and you will learn the ropes as your book is being published. Authors who publish with Alkira or Escarpment Publishing, for instance, get educational material on aspects of publishing and are included in the project management and decision-making process. By the time their book is published, they are well set to take the leap into self-publishing their next book if they choose to.

If you are a hobby writer with a decent budget, then I'd skip the legacy route and aim for a hybrid publisher with a strong editorial department that will make sure your book is the best it can possibly be. If your book isn't accepted by a hybrid publisher, then your book needs more work. If that's the case, you'll need to decide how important quality is to you. You can self-publish or pay for a publishing service with the book as it is, but wouldn't it be better to work with an editor and improve your book first?

There's no point in publishing and promoting a book of inferior quality, yet authors continue to do so in the misguided notion that they are 'saving money' by not working with professional editors and book designers. Scrimping on such things is a false economy. Though publishing quality doesn't guarantee sales by itself—because promotion (and luck) influences sales—all the quality promotions in the world won't result in good sales for a shoddy book.

Finding the Right Publisher

Finding the right publisher could take you a lot of time, but the answer to the question of how you go about finding them is quite simple. It can be answered in one word: research.

- Search for a list of publishers—by genre or publishing method. Find a list made by an independent body that rates publishing businesses, but check their evaluation criteria so you know what they're evaluating. The Alliance of Independent Authors has a list that rates hybrid and self-publishing services. This is a good way to avoid known scammers.
- Choose a publisher who publishes your genre and look at their website. What kind of publisher are they? Are they transparent about their services and charges? How do their charges

compare to others offering similar services?

- Who runs the business? Who will you be working with? What is their background?
- Look at their blog posts and videos of the people who run the business. Are these people you will be able to trust?
- Do you like the covers of their books?
- Look at reviews and endorsements of the business and of the books.
- Read one of their books. Is it quality?
- Make a shortlist of potential publishers, read their submission guidelines and make submissions. If you get offered a deal, check the contract carefully, then make your decision.

Understanding the Publishing Process

Once a book has been accepted by a publisher and the contract is signed, many authors wonder what comes next. Publishing is a complex, multi-step process, and understanding each stage can help you prepare, stay on track, set realistic expectations and work more effectively with your publisher. While it may feel like a lot, each stage is designed to ensure your book is polished, professional and ready to find its audience. Good communication, flexibility, and trust in the expertise of your publishing team will make the journey smoother and more rewarding.

While the specifics vary between publishing houses, the general sequence of events is quite consistent. Below is a step-by-step breakdown of what happens after your manuscript has been accepted for publication.

Editing

How much editing is done by the publisher or requested by the publisher depends on the kind of publisher, but the editing is always completed before formatting begins. If they haven't already done so, the author should write any dedication, acknowledgments or notes to the readers they want included in the book and insert them into the manuscript before the copy edit has been completed.

Front and Back Matter

The publisher inserts the title page, copyright page and back matter (about the author, note on their other books and so on) into the manuscript. These components complete the full interior of the book.

Editorial Reviews Sought

Either the publisher or the author will order professional editorial reviews to gain endorsements for the back cover and the book's product page.

Interior Formatting for Print

The interior of the book is formatted for print. This involves setting the correct margins, font choices, chapter headings, spacing and page numbers. The result is a professionally typeset file that meets industry standards.

Proofreading

The proofread is a quality control step to catch any remaining errors before the book goes to print and digital formatting.

Back Cover Description

Meanwhile, the back cover description is written— either by the author or publishing team or a combination of both.

Ebook Cover Design

The design process begins with the creation of the ebook cover. This version is designed to be eye-catching in thumbnail size, optimised for online stores. Authors working with a professional designer in an author-funded publishing model will be involved in approving concept directions and final designs.

Assignment of ISBNs

The publisher assigns ISBNs (International Standard Book Number) for the print and ebook editions. Each format of the book requires a separate ISBN to distinguish it in global book databases and ensure distribution through retailers and libraries.

Print Cover Creation

The designer creates the full print cover (front, spine and back). The spine width is calculated based on the interior file, and the back cover description and barcode are added. Editorial review excerpts go on the back cover.

Research Categories and Keywords

The publisher researches and selects the best BISAC (Book Industry Standards and Communications) categories, keywords and metadata tags for the book. These are vital for ensuring the book is discoverable in online searches and is properly categorised by genre and theme.

Upload Files to Printer

Once the cover and interior are complete, the print-ready files are uploaded to the printer. Indie publishers use global print-on-demand platforms, such as Ingram Spark, to print and distribute books to online retailers such as Amazon and Booktopia. Mainstream publishers use offset printing for large print runs.

Ebook Formatting

The ebook version is formatted separately to the print version, with different design requirements for reflowable text, clickable links and navigation features like a functional table of contents.

Uploading to Ebook Platforms

Once formatted, the ebook files are uploaded to platforms such as Kindle Direct Publishing (KDP), Draft2Digital and others. These platforms distribute the ebook to various online retailers, including Amazon, Apple Books, Kobo and Barnes & Noble.

Appearance in Online Bookstores

Your ebook and print copies will appear in online bookstores once the uploads are processed and approved. This typically happens one to two weeks after file upload for the paperback on Amazon and later for other online retailers. Mainstream publishers follow their usual protocols for getting books into bookstores.

Book Promotion

Book promotion begins as soon as possible, with the author building their online author platform—social media accounts and website. Then, once the book is available for pre-order, the promotional activities ramp up, culminating on release day. This includes announcements on social media, email newsletters, blog posts, launch events, giveaways, advertisements and outreach to reviewers. The author and publisher work together to build momentum and generate interest in the book. Months after publication, cut-price promotions for the ebook may be organised to keep the sales momentum going.

Is My Book Worth the Cost of Paying for Publishing?

At some point in your writing journey, you're going to ask yourself, 'Is my book worth the effort and/or cost of publishing?' This is likely to be after you've had some feedback that indicates that you have a lot of work to do to get the book into shape.

Editing costs are considerable and comprise the major expense for producing a quality book, so you may baulk when faced with paying thousands of dollars to have your book fully edited. And publishing and promotional costs can run into the thousands.

Once you've had it edited, you'll want to take the next step, but unless you get a legacy publishing deal—which is a long shot—you're looking at paying for publishing. If you can afford it, great, no problem. But if you can't afford to do it well, then it's a good idea to ask yourself if you can afford to *not* do it well. Will publishing something that isn't as good as it should be achieve your publishing goals? Sometimes, it may be best to shelve the book, celebrate that you have learned a lot about writing and then write a different book.

I met an author who wrote five different books before one was accepted by a legacy publisher. He never wanted to pay for publishing, so he just kept learning and improving his writing. This was the way all authors worked before the advent of desktop publishing, print on demand, modern ebook technology and Amazon's KDP and Lightning Source (Ingram Spark) distribution outlets.

I have three shelved books on my computer. I could publish them, but there's no point because all of them require more work, and even if I do the work, they will never be more than mediocre books. I decided to save my money on those three.

To help you decide, have the manuscript appraised and ask the editor for their ruthless opinion as to its worthiness for publication in terms of your goals. If you've already had it edited—and editing should start with an appraisal—and you're unsure whether you should invest more money in it, consider getting an appraisal from a different editor. I've had several books come to me that authors swear have been 'fully edited' yet the editor had missed some very major flaws. The second appraisal, though it costs, could save you a lot of money in the long run.

If cost is an issue, then ruling out investing in something that may not be worth investing in is a good move. Paying out a couple of hundred dollars may save you from paying out several grand on something that is never going to do well. If you don't have beta readers able to give you critical feedback, then having a couple of appraisals before choosing an editor is a good idea. Choose the one with the most criticism!

If editing and publishing the book will be a stretch financially, then ask yourself how important it is for you to hold the completed book in your hand. Is it something you're willing to stretch for?

The best way to make an objective decision on this is to engage a publishing professional willing to be ruthlessly honest with you, and you must be willing to ditch the project. If you're not willing to ditch the project, then the book is worth publishing simply because you want it published.

Will I Pay Off My Costs?

Many authors try the mainstream route because the publisher pays for the publishing. Apart from editing costs—and I recommend paying for at least a manuscript appraisal before submitting your manuscript—the author isn't laying out a lot of money. But a mainstream deal is no guarantee of big sales or getting anything like a living wage for the hours you've taken to write your book—most authors never get either of these. Mainstream publishers don't pay royalties until the book sales have paid off the advance payment, though these days, you're lucky to even get an advance.

According to an Australian Society of Authors (ASA) 2021 survey, 58% of respondents indicated they received no advance for their work, and 80.6% of respondents received advances under $5,000. Only 13% of respondents reported receiving an advance over $10,000. [6]

Data from BookScan on the top ten mainstream publishers found that 66% of books sell fewer than 1,000 copies, and a mere 2% sell more than 5,000. [7]

---

6. https://www.asauthors.org.au/news/what-you-need-to-know-about-book-advances/

7. https://johnmjennings.com/a-shockingly-small-percentage-

'When Penguin Random House attempted to acquire Simon & Schuster, the Department of Justice sued to stop the merger. The case went to court, and publishing secrets were brought to light … One of the classic findings from the trial was that most authors are not earning out the advance. … most books, some 85%, fail. A book that "fails" is one that simply didn't live up to the publisher's expectations.' https://www.authormedia.com/publishing-industry-secrets-revealed-at-the-penguin-random-house-trial*

And that was for mainstream books that have been selected because the publishers think they can sell them. If you get an advance that covers what you paid out in editing, you will have covered your costs. If there's no advance, you'll have to wait and see.

In the self-publishing sphere, The Independent Author Income Survey, March 27, 2023, conducted for the Alliance of Independent Authors, states: [8]

---

of-books-account-for-most-sales/

8. https://selfpublishingadvice.org/wp-content/uploads/2023/04/The-Independent-Author-Income-Survey-updated-FINAL-17-04-23.pdf?

The survey focused on gaining an improved understanding of self-published authors' incomes and income-related strategies. Self-published authors were defined as individuals who had self-published at least one book and who spent at least 50% of their working time on writing and publishing activities.

- *41% of self-publisher respondents had earned more than $20,000 as authors during the past two years.*
- *The median writing and self-publishing-related income in 2022 of all self-publishers responding was $12,749.*

According to this, most self-publishing (including pay-to-publish) authors will recoup their costs and earn a modest income, but this data is only relevant to those who spend 50% of their working time on writing and publishing. These authors run their writing and publishing as a business and have solid promotional strategies, but in my experience, most authors don't do this, as they have day jobs and families taking up their time. In my experience, the following data is more likely to be the reality for most pay-to-publish authors:

It's hard to compete in the book market and promote the title. Most self-published books

rarely get the attention of the readers, and this
reflects sales and revenue figures:
- *Over 90% of self-published books sell under 100*
  copies during their lifetime.
- *The average self-published author will earn under*
  $1,000 from book sales during the year.
- *The average self-published title will sell around*
  250 copies during its lifetime. [9]

So the answer to whether you will pay off your costs depends on how you approach your writing: as a long-term business or as a hobby, what your initial costs are, how much effort and professional assistance you put into it, and how well your book sells—which has to do with how big your possible readership is, how well you promote it, and luck.

These figures may leave you wondering if it's worth writing and publishing a book, but writing has always been a few-earn-most-don't occupation, so poor odds for financial success as an author is nothing new. This is why authors say that you must love writing to be an author. You need to get satisfaction from the writing process itself and enjoy your interaction with your readers, so that if you don't meet your financial aims, at least it isn't wasted time and money. When it comes to having

9. https://wordsratec.com/book-sales-statistics/

realistic expectations as to paying off one's costs, the trick is to see financial success as the icing on the cake rather than the main reason for writing. Remind yourself that adding quality to the trillions of books out there is more important than selling millions of books. It's certainly what's best for your readers.

Work out a budget, see if you can get a good result for what you can afford or are prepared to spend, and then decide: Is this book worth it? Or can I do better?

The Value of Your Book

Though not everyone can write books that are top quality, we can all write a book that can then be worked on until it's good enough to publish. Editors make their living from helping authors to make their books the best they can possibly be, and with the right kind of help, you can produce a quality book that will, at the very least, surprise your friends and family. Certainly, for those with more modest goals than becoming a bestseller or literary wonder, it's likely their book will meet their goals. At Alkira Publishing, we help authors to do exactly that.

The best books have more than beautiful prose and tight editing; they also have a depth of insight into the human spirit. They move you. The characters are written such that the reader shares their hopes and fears and loves and losses. Such books draw us into the story in such a way that we live the character's lives, and their lives enrich us. They may even illuminate something about ourselves. This is the sort of quality that makes a book literary fiction.

Not all books fit this category, of course, and neither should they. Some books are designed to be action rather than character-driven, and in such books little time is spent on the character's emotional reactions to events. The best books, however—the ones you remember, tell your friends about, and for which you leave rave reviews—have a strong plot that includes some action, depth of character, and some insight into the human condition, and, of course, they're well written. Even if you're writing genre fiction, your book is improved by the qualities that make us label something as literary fiction; but how do we give our books the best chance of moving readers in this way?

I've covered those elements previously in this book, but just before you move onto publication is a good time to look at your book again and reevaluate it in terms of the key points.

Excellent books have an aim for the protagonist and something or someone (the antagonist) to get in the way of your protagonist achieving their aim. Without this, you don't have any dramatic tension, and without tension, a book is dull. Good books have conflict or mystery or suspense or tasks to complete or relationship issues to resolve.

They also have characters who are real, who are complex, who have hopes and fears, strengths and weaknesses we can relate to, and who react to the events they experience and grow from them. The deeper the author dives into a character's mind, heart and motivations, the greater the book.

Insight that infuses the writing can make a book truly special. When it flows naturally from the author as a person, drawn from their life experience and values, it marks the author's voice, that special quality that makes a book unique. Authors with strong voices have the courage to bare their souls to the world.

From the author's point of view, insight comes into writing when we dig deep into ourselves and enter our characters and story fully as we write. Our heart should pound as our character battles their foe and soften when they pick up a baby or a puppy. When we write a character walking into a tomb (for example), we should live that moment ourselves so we can write exactly how it feels to step into that cool and morbid interior—or perhaps we don't find it morbid; perhaps our character finds tombs inspiring.

Author voice and insightful writing also come

from trusting that we do have some depth of insight and that we only need to allow it to come out naturally. No need to force anything. And it comes from not separating ourselves from our stories. That's how we develop voice as an author, our special take on the world that is completely unique.

All great authors acknowledge the assistance of their editors and publishers, and the less experience as an author you have, the more you need professional assistance. If you're trying to minimise costs, it's tempting to cut a professional service somewhere, but then you have a lower-value product.

The Personal Value of Your Book

Your book, no matter how it turns out, no matter how many you sell or whether anyone likes it or not, is still a good book for you because you needed to write that book, work on it and have it published. You had a story you needed to tell, and if you worked on it with a professional to make it the best it can be, then you have a product that is worthy of publication. Even if that book doesn't make anyone's top ten reads for the year, you will have learned a lot during the process of writing it. Maybe now you can write a better one, or maybe you are better able to see what your story means for you, why it was important that you wrote it. Maybe you needed to write it to sort out something in your mind, or to assimilate or move on from an event in your life. These are all excellent reasons to write a book and feel satisfaction at its completion.

In a time when publication is open to more people than ever before, book writing and publication has a wider purpose than it did when only a select few could publish. Writing for personal growth or simply to leave the story of your life for your family are just as good reasons to write as any other. Whether or not that story ever gets to a publishable standard depends on your willingness to work on it and to pay professionals to help you. If, after you have done that, however, your book doesn't resonate with others, that is no reason to feel you have failed. It's still a good book for you because you wrote it, and the process of doing so benefited you; you wouldn't have done it unless you needed to.

The process of developing your author voice can be most illuminating from a self-knowledge perspective, and that is a valuable journey to take, regardless of sales or quality.

My Mission as an Editor and Publisher

I see my mission for this part of my life as helping people to write their stories well and to sculpt them into something of a publishable standard. Some books will achieve the 'truly awesome' label, but most, despite my best efforts, will not reach the pinnacle of literary quality. And that's perfectly okay. The important thing for authors is that they've written their story and done it to the best of their ability, and that is enough. All stories have value. It's my job to help my authors make their stories as readable as possible, and if you come to me for help, I'll push you to go as deep as you can into yourself and your experiences to encourage you to reveal your greatness. Not only that, but as a line editor, I will turn poor or pedestrian prose into something of quality. In other words, I will give you your best shot at making your novel or memoir truly great.

The Submission Process

Is Your Book Ready for Submission?

The biggest issue I see as a publisher reading submissions is authors who rush into publication before the book is ready. Often that translates into wanting a publisher to publish their book immediately or self-publishing a book that needs more work. Writing a good book takes time, especially your first one. Publishing also takes time if you are to ensure that the book is a quality product. Remember also that you need sufficient time to promote your book before publication day.

The first question you need to answer before submitting your manuscript to an agent or publisher of any kind is: Is your book ready for submission? Here's a tip: If you haven't had some professional feedback on your book, it isn't ready. An author can never know what it is like for someone to read their book without knowing everything the author knows and without having the author's vision in their minds. As this is how everyone begins their reading of your book, you need to know how it comes across to others before it is finalised. The best way to get that feedback is from a professional editor. The second-best way is beta reading, and I've talked about that before.

The other important factor in knowing if it's ready for submission is whether you feel the story is complete. You need to feel sure about this, because there is nothing worse for a publisher (including you, if you're doing it yourself) than an author who keeps wanting to change the manuscript even after the editing and formatting has been done. At a certain point, you have to say to yourself, 'Yes, it's done,' and then leave it alone.

Sometimes authors tell me they want to change something even after they've signed off on the manuscript as being completed, and it's a word here or there that doesn't make any difference to the readers' perception of the overall story. Some even want to make changes that make the writing worse.

The story is finished when you feel you have written it to the best of your ability. If you're submitting it to a publisher rather than self-publishing it, however, then you need to be prepared to do more work on the book if the publisher requires it. Remember, you don't know what you don't know and can't see what you don't see. You may think your manuscript is finished, but a publisher can still tell you it needs more work.

Most publishers will just say no. They'll send you a copy-and-paste rejection notice, with no feedback at all. Giving feedback isn't their job.

Alkira Publishing is a rare kind of publisher in that if we see a submission that is clearly not ready for publication but has the potential to be a quality book with a bit more work, we offer to help the author work on it. Some we reject outright, but if an author is willing to work on it more under the guidance of our editorial team, then we give them that opportunity. Other publishers, especially legacy publishers, will not give you that option. Nor do you get a chance to resubmit, so you want to submit your best effort.

Researching and Making the Submission

Choose who you will submit to carefully. You are wasting your time and the publisher's time if you submit to everyone. The single most important thing is to follow the publisher or agent's submission process exactly. Their submission guidelines are there for a reason; they facilitate the publisher's process. Publishers get a lot of submissions, and they don't have time to wade through submissions that don't follow their guidelines. Submitting in a way that isn't what a publisher requests is unprofessional, shows a lack of respect, and in large publishing houses may even result in your submission being rejected without being read.

Specifically:

- Look at the publisher's website and check that they publish your genre.
- Check what kinds of books they are looking for. Sometimes they will say they are not accepting a particular genre now. Pay attention to that, and don't submit if that's your genre. They won't look at it, and they won't hold it until later.
- Make a shortlist of suitable publishers and agents, ones whose listed titles indicate that

your book might be a good fit for them.

- Some publishers list the names of specific editors and what they are presently looking for. Mention the editor and say why you think they might like your book in your query letter (or message if it's an online form).
- In your message say why you think the publisher would be a good fit for your book. Make sure this is specific to each publisher and agent. Avoid generic submissions, which are obvious. Impress with your understanding of the publisher's mission.
- If you're filling in an online contact form rather than sending an email to an email address, include everything listed in Chapter 46 as necessary for the query letter.
- Sometimes you can email a query letter. In that case put it in the body of the email—unless they ask for an attachment.
- Do not include your manuscript unless asked for it.
- Do not include a cover design or character images. You are submitting to people who not only have an imagination but also want your book to spark it, not an image.
- Most important: Read their submission page carefully, and do not diverge from what they

request. If asked for your manuscript, make sure that it is formatted exactly as requested.

Should I Follow up if I Don't Hear Back?

Generally, only follow up if you didn't get an email acknowledging receipt of the submission. You need to allow the publisher or agent time to process your submission, and it can take months for larger publishers to get back to you. But check their website—many list response times. If it's been, say, eight to twelve weeks, and they allow follow-ups, a polite nudge is okay. But never be demanding. Publishing can be a slow process, and sometimes silence means no.

How to Write a Book Description That Hooks Readers

You've written your book—tens of thousands of words, maybe more. And now comes the part that makes many writers freeze.

How do you Describe Your Book in Just 180 Words, and Why?

A book description (or 'blurb') is one of the most important tools you have for drawing readers in. Whether you're self-publishing or submitting to agents, this short paragraph can make the difference between a reader clicking *Buy Now*—or not.

Why 180 Words?

Most online platforms show only the first few

lines of your book description unless the reader clicks 'Read more'. This means your hook—the opening line—has to work hard. Think of it like a movie trailer for your book. You don't have time to include every subplot or character. You only have time to make the reader *care enough to want more*.

What Makes a Good Book Description?

A strong book description usually includes four key elements:

- **The hook**—an opening line that sparks curiosity or tension.
- **The premise**—the emotional core or 'what it's about underneath'.
- **The characters**—who the story follows and what drives them.
- **The conflict**—what's at stake? What stands in their way? And most importantly: It must reflect the tone and voice of the book. Is your story whimsical? Dark and thrilling? Meditative and lyrical? Your blurb should feel like a glimpse into that world—not just a summary.

Language Matters

Think active verbs, vivid imagery and emotional cues. Avoid passive constructions or vague descriptions like: 'This is a story about love and loss'. Instead, say something like:

> *After a mysterious illness leaves her mute, seventeen-year-old Liora discovers she can hear people's unspoken thoughts—but only when they're lying.*

Now we know:
- who the main character is
- what makes her unique
- what the story's conflict might involve
- that it's likely YA with speculative elements

Clarity and specificity will always do more for you than trying to be poetic or cryptic.

A Useful Formula

See if you can make your book fit this formula. It doesn't matter if it doesn't, but it may be a useful exercise to help you clarify what you need to put into the description.

When [*identity*] [*protagonist name*] [*does something*], [*something happens*]. Now, with [*time limit/restrictions*], [*protagonist*] must [*do something brave*] to [*accomplish great achievement*] / or [*sacrifice high stakes*].

Writing for Real People

Sometimes writers think the blurb has to impress reviewers, agents or other writers. But remember— you're writing for readers. A potential reader scanning dozens of titles on their screen doesn't want complexity—they want intrigue, emotion and a sense of the journey you're about to take them on.

Don't be afraid to revise your description many times. Read it aloud. Trim the fluff. The first version is never the final version.

Your Blurb is a Marketing Tool

Once you've written a great blurb, don't just tuck it away on your book page. Use it on social media. Break it into teaser lines for posts. Create a 50-word version for your newsletter or author bio.

In fact, here's a challenge: Try writing a 50-word version of your book description. It will help you distil the essence of your story—and you might be surprised by what it reveals about your central theme.

Writing a book description is hard—but it's also an opportunity. It invites you to clarify your story's heart, sharpen your message and connect directly with your future readers. That's powerful. Whether you're just starting to think about marketing or you're about to hit publish, take the time to get this part right. It's worth it.

How to Write a Query Letter That Gets Read

Whether you're approaching a literary agent, a publisher or a reviewer, a query letter is your novel's first impression. This one-page letter/email is your foot in the door—and it needs to shine. Done well, it piques interest, shows professionalism and opens the path to publication or review. Done poorly, it closes doors before they even open.

Not every agent or publisher requests a query letter these days, so make sure you check their submission guidelines before sending your query. Many now have a form to fill in with the exact information they need, but at some point in your author journey, you'll probably want to contact reviewers, and a query letter is the way to do it if there is no form on their website.

This chapter outlines what to include, what

to avoid and how to craft a compelling query that respects the protocols of the industry while showcasing your unique voice.

The Purpose of a Query Letter

A query letter has a clear job: to convince the recipient they want to read your manuscript. It's a sales pitch, yes—but not a hard sell. It's a professional, concise introduction that provides:

- a brief hook or summary of your novel
- information about your manuscript (title, genre, word count)
- a short author bio (relevant credentials or platform)
- a demonstration that you've done your research

A query letter is not a synopsis, a life story or a place to plead for exceptions. It's your opportunity to be taken seriously as a writer.

Do Your Homework First

Before writing a single sentence, **research the person or company you're querying**. As I said in the chapter on the submission process, read the agent's or publisher's submission guidelines thoroughly:

- Are they currently open for submissions?
- Do they accept your genre?
- Do they prefer a query-only email or a query with sample pages?
- Do they want a synopsis attached? Pasted in? Not at all?
- Do they specify a word count limit or a preferred tone?

Ignoring these guidelines is one of the quickest ways to get your query deleted unread. Mentioning that you've followed their guidelines shows professionalism and respect.

If you're submitting to a reviewer, ensure they cover your genre and are accepting books for review. Respect their preferences for format (physical copy vs digital), lead time and audience.

The Ideal Structure of a Query Letter

A standard query letter should fit neatly onto one A4 page (or under 400 words in an email). Here's a reliable structure:

The Greeting

Always address the person by name—*Dear Ms Johnson*, not *To whom it may concern*. This signals you've done your research and aren't mass-sending.

If you're unsure of gender or pronouns, *Dear Jordan Taylor* works fine.

The Hook or Blurb Paragraph

Start strong. This is a one-to-three sentence hook that gives a taste of your novel's premise. Think of it like the back-cover blurb—your chance to entice the reader into your fictional world.

Focus on:
- your protagonist
- the central conflict
- the stakes

Avoid vagueness like, 'This novel explores love and betrayal.' Be specific:

> *When sixteen-year-old Mara discovers her brother is working for the enemy, she must choose between family loyalty and saving her village from destruction.*

This paragraph should evoke tone and genre while showcasing your storytelling voice.

Manuscript Details

In a new paragraph, give the basics:
- title (in capitals)
- genre
- word count (rounded to the nearest 1,000 words)
- target audience (if appropriate)

Example: *SHADOWSONG is a completed 85,000-word young-adult fantasy novel for fans of Holly Black and Laini Taylor.*

If it's part of a series, mention that it can stand alone but has series potential. Avoid promising 'the next bestseller'.

Author Bio

Keep it short. Include:
- relevant writing credentials (e.g., publications, awards, writing degrees)
- platform or reach (especially for nonfiction or memoir)

- personal details only if they are directly connected to the story

Example: *I hold an MA in Creative Writing, and my short stories have appeared in* Meanjin *and* Overland. *Like my protagonist, I grew up in a remote community on the south coast of New South Wales.*

If you're unpublished, don't apologise—just skip to relevant facts or state briefly that this is your debut.

Why You're Submitting to Them

This is optional but powerful. A single sentence showing you've chosen them for a reason can make a big difference.

Example: *I'm querying you because of your interest in character-driven speculative fiction, and because you represent several authors whose work I admire.*

Or: *Your recent callout for Australian fantasy authors resonated with me, and I believe my novel aligns with your list.*

Keep it specific and sincere—generic flattery backfires.

Closing and Contact Details

Close politely:

Thank you for considering my submission. The full manuscript is available on request.

Then include your contact info if sending by email:

- full name
- email address
- phone (optional)
- website or social media (if professional and relevant)

Tips for Tone and Style

- **Professional, not pushy.** Avoid hype or desperation. Don't say, 'This will be the next *Harry Potter*' or 'You'd be foolish not to represent me'.
- **Confident, not arrogant.** You don't need to apologise for submitting, but also avoid boasting.
- **Clear and concise.** Use plain language. Avoid jargon, purple prose or overly complicated sentences.
- **Proofread.** Typos suggest carelessness. Read aloud before sending.

What Not to Include

- your age, unless it's relevant (e.g., you're writing YA and you're a teen)
- detailed backstory about your writing journey
- a full synopsis (unless requested)
- quotes from friends or beta readers
- irrelevant personal information
- attachments they didn't ask for

And never send mass queries. Personalise each one, even if just by name and relevance.

Follow the Submission Guidelines Exactly

Every agent, publisher and reviewer will have their own preferences. Follow them to the letter. If they want the first five pages pasted into the email, do that. If they want no attachments, don't send any. If they say they'll respond only if interested, don't chase them after two weeks.

This shows you can work within the industry's expectations—a key trait they're looking for in an author.

Summary

A good query letter does three things:
- It introduces your book clearly and enticingly.
- It presents you as a competent, professional writer.
- It shows you've taken the time to tailor your approach.

You don't need to be flashy. You just need to be clear, courteous and compelling.

The query letter is a bridge between your story and the people who can help bring it into the world. Craft it with care, and it may just be the key that opens the door.

Example

Subject: Query: *THE DARWIN ELEVATOR* – Science Fiction Novel

Dear Ms Megibow,

From your profile on *Publishers' Marketplace*, I see that we share a love for John Scalzi's *Old Man's War*. I am contacting you for representation of my science fiction novel, *THE DARWIN ELEVATOR*. The manuscript is complete at 130,000 words and can stand alone or become a series.

Skyler is immune to a disease that has wiped out most of humanity. Only one place on Earth is safe for those not immune: Darwin, Australia, where a space elevator of alien origin suppresses the disease. Trapped in the city, the ragged citizens of Darwin rely on food grown aboard orbiting space stations to survive. They rely on scavengers like Skyler for everything else. With a small crew of fellow 'immunes', Skyler leads missions into the dangerous world beyond Darwin's safe zone, searching for the useful relics of old Earth. Spare parts, ammunition, books—for a price, Skyler will find it.

When a reviled political leader hires him to retrieve information from a long-abandoned telescope and smuggle the data to scientists living in orbit, Skyler is thrust into the middle of a conspiracy. The telescope data proves another alien ship is approaching Earth. While trying to keep the discovery secret, Skyler's employer sparks a bloody coup, led by a faction hell-bent on total control of the Darwin Elevator. As the uprising spirals into all-out war and the alien ship nears Earth, Skyler must risk everything to protect a secret he barely understands.

I learned the art of creating fictional worlds while designing sci-fi video games, such as *Aliens vs*

Predator: Extinction and *Metal Fatigue*. These titles featured intricate stories and complex characters. I feel that this experience, and my lifetime passion for the genre, has transferred well to the medium of the novel.

Thank you for your time and consideration.

Sincerely,

Jason M Hough

Key Elements Demonstrated:

- **Personalisation:** The letter opens by referencing the agent's interests, showing that the author has done their research.
- **Compelling hook:** The initial paragraph introduces a unique premise that piques interest.
- **Concise synopsis:** The body provides a clear and engaging summary of the plot, highlighting stakes and conflicts.
- **Author credentials:** The author mentions relevant experience in storytelling and worldbuilding, lending credibility.
- **Professional tone:** The letter maintains a respectful and businesslike tone throughout.

Tips for Working with a Publisher

Publishing a book is a partnership. Whether you're working with a mainstream publisher or an author-funded publisher, your ability to build a respectful, professional relationship can have a direct impact on the success of your book—and on how enjoyable the process feels.

This chapter offers guidance for navigating that relationship with confidence and clarity so you can focus on what matters: getting your book into the world in its best possible form.

Choose a Publisher You Can Trust

The basis of any good relationship is trust. The publisher trusts that you will do what's required of you, and you need to trust that your publisher knows what they are doing and will make the best decisions for your book. This is why choosing your publisher carefully is so important. As I said in Chapter 40 on choosing a publisher:

- **Research the publisher**: Check their reputation, previous titles, author testimonials and distribution reach.
- **Look for professionalism**: Are their books well designed? Are their communications clear and respectful?
- **Pay attention to red flags**: Poor-quality books, vague contracts, overly glowing promises or high-pressure sales tactics are warning signs.

The more trust you have in your publisher's expertise, the easier the process will be. You don't want to be in a situation where you're questioning every decision they make. That makes for a difficult experience for both you and the publisher.

The Contract

Before you begin any work with a publisher—
mainstream or author-paid—read the contract
carefully. If you don't understand something, ask
questions or seek legal advice from a publishing-savvy
lawyer or a writers' organisation in your country.
Look for:

- What rights you're granting (territorial, print,
  digital, audio, etc.)
- How and when you'll be paid (advances,
  royalties, percentages)
- What you're expected to do (edits,
  approvals, marketing)
- What the publisher is responsible for (editing,
  design, distribution, promotion)
- Termination clauses (how you or the publisher
  can end the agreement)

If you're paying a publisher, your contract should
clearly define what services you are purchasing,
what creative input you'll have and who owns the
rights at the end of the process.

If you don't feel comfortable with the terms,
don't sign until you do. A reputable publisher won't
pressure you to rush. Once you've signed the contract,
it's time to let go of control and trust the process.

Know Who Makes the Decisions

Mainstream Publishers

- You usually don't have any say on cover design, typesetting, pricing or marketing.
- Your input may be invited, especially on things like the cover brief or title, but the publisher will make final decisions based on marketability.
- This isn't personal—it's business. Publishers rely on data, market trends and professional experience to make decisions that will give your book the best chance of success.

Author-Paid/Hybrid Publishers

- You are the client, so you often have more input or approval rights, especially around the cover and layout.
- However, that doesn't mean they will or should act on every suggestion you make. Your publisher still knows what sells and what looks professional. Knowing the ins and outs of the publishing business is their area of expertise, so trust their guidance. Don't listen to friends and family over your professional team.

Be willing to listen and learn. Where you are given a say, respect the publisher's guidance. They want your book to succeed too.

Communicate Clearly and Professionally

Clear, respectful communication is one of the biggest factors in a smooth publishing experience. Here's how to do it well:

- **Keep emails short**: Publishers are busy. Don't send essays. Aim for a maximum of two or three short paragraphs.
- **Use dot points for requests**: This makes it easy for the publisher to respond point-by-point.
- **Keep all communication in one email thread**: Don't start a new email for each question or thought.
- **Use clear subject lines**: For example, 'Final proof edits for *Book Title*' or 'Cover feedback – *Book Title*'.
- **Be polite and professional**: Avoid all caps, excessive exclamation marks and emotionally charged language. Publishing is emotional, but it's also business.

Example Email

Subject: Cover feedback – *Wings of Shadow*
Hi [Publisher Name],
Thanks for sending through the cover options.
I appreciate the work that's gone into these.
Here are my notes:
Option 2 is my preferred layout.
Could we explore a darker colour palette?
The subtitle text is a bit hard to read on a mobile—can it be bolder?
Thanks again!
Warm regards, Tahlia

Be a Collaborative Partner

Publishing is not just about handing your manuscript over and waiting for a launch date. It's a joint effort.

Here's how to be a good collaborator:

- **Meet your deadlines**: If you're given edits or approvals, return them by the agreed date.
- **Respond promptly to emails**: Within two to three business days is standard.
- **Be open to feedback**: Every author needs editing. It doesn't mean your book isn't good— it means your publisher wants it to be the best

it can be.

- **Be solutions-focused**: If something's not working, approach it with a 'How can we fix this together?' mindset, not blame.

Balance Trust with Advocacy

Publishing requires a delicate balance:
- Trust your publisher's expertise, especially in areas where they know more than you (cover design, marketing, typesetting, etc.)
- Advocate for your vision if something feels truly out of alignment—but do so respectfully and with a willingness to find middle ground.

Ask yourself:

Is this a personal preference, or does it affect the professionalism or success of the book?

If it's just a preference, consider letting it go.

Remember the Shared Goal

Whether you're paying for services or being traditionally published, your publisher wants your book to succeed. You're not on opposite sides—you're on the same team.

Good publishers:

- care about the quality of your book
- want you to be proud of the final result
- rely on your satisfaction and success for their reputation

Good authors:
- respect the expertise they're hiring
- are open to collaboration
- stay professional even when emotions run high

Step-by-Step Self-publishing

This is a very brief rundown of what is involved in self-publishing, so you have some idea of the scope of knowledge you'll need to obtain.

1. Join the Alliance of Independent Authors to get reliable independent support.
2. Study how to self-publish. Research:
   - What is an ISBN, and how do I get one?
   - The difference between Ingram Spark (IS) and KDP
   - How to format a book for paperback and ebook (or pay a professional to do it for you)
   - How to publish an ebook? (I suggest Draft2Digital and Amazon's KDP as your platforms)

- How to use Amazon categories and keywords
- How to write a book blurb
- What makes a good book cover?
- Book marketing for self-published authors

3. Research to find your editor, proofreader, cover designer and book formatter. Discuss their availability with them.

4. Decide on a publication date and set up some kind of project management system to make sure everything gets done on time.

5. Study book promotion, make a plan and work out a promotion timeline.

6. Add a copyright page and front and back matter to your book.

7. Have the book professionally and comprehensively edited and proofread.

8. Write a book description for the back cover and get your editor to check it.

9. Arrange editorial reviews for the back cover. Paid review sites are a necessity to get the kind of quality and 'name' you want for your back cover and product page reviews.

10. Begin finding readers who will read and review your book on Amazon. There are paid services that will find reviewers for you.

11. Choose a printer/distributor for your print copies and set up an account. The main options for commercial novels are IS and KDP. Lulu is an option if interior colour images are an important part of the book.

Decide if you want to have worldwide distribution for the book by using IS as your printer/distributor or have a lesser distribution with Amazon KDP.

- Amazon is simpler to set up, but the return to you per book is less than for IS, and the book will only be available outside of Amazon stores if you choose 'expanded distribution' during setup. Even then, it will not be the width of distribution offered by IS. Also, the amount you get per book for their expanded distribution is less than if you sell a book printed by IS in the same place. However, you will never get an 'Out of Stock' sign against your book on Amazon.

- In general, those who want full worldwide distribution and the possibility of brick-and-mortar bookstores being able to stock it choose IS. Those who want the easiest method of self-publishing, are okay with a more limited distribution, happy mainly selling through Amazon stores, and don't care that a brick-and-mortar bookstore will probably not stock it (because Amazon is the publisher) choose KDP.

- If you don't live in the UK or the USA, getting author copies from Amazon will be expensive, so it's best to use IS.
- Lulu has the best quality interior colour prints. Their books are, however, more expensive to print and therefore to purchase. They also have a lesser distribution than IS, though your book will still be available in major stores.

12. Get your ISBN and add it to your copyright page.

- You can get free ISBNs from IS and KDP, but they will own the ISBN and be the publisher, not you. For KDP, your book publisher name on your product page will read 'Independently published'.
- IS offer discounted rates if you want to own your own ISBN.

13. If you're planning to write several books and want to take a professional approach, then you (or your business name) will want to be listed as the publisher on book databases. The best practice then is to get your own ISBN. For that, you must create an account with Bowker Identifiers in whatever name you want to call yourself as a publisher; then you can purchase them from there.

14. Get an ebook cover designed. Don't try to do it yourself.
15. Look at the size options for paperback and choose a size.
16. Get the interior formatted for paperback (or learn how to do it yourself).
17. Get a template for the paperback cover from your printer (IS or KDP Print).
18. Get your cover designer to design the paperback cover on the template and exported to the printer's specifications.
19. Research the best categories and keywords to use during title setup.
20. Decide whether you want it available for pre-order and what your timeframe will be.
21. Set up the title with the printer and upload the files at least six weeks before the publication date, so you have time to check a physical copy before ordering a large number for your book launch.
22. Approve the eproof if it looks correct.
23. Order a physical proof. Check that it has printed without errors.
24. Arrange to get author copies for your

book launch.

25. Set up the ebook on your chosen platform(s).

26. Have a book launch on or soon after your publication day.

It looks simple, doesn't it? Only twenty-six points. But of course, each point involves a great deal of learning, decision making and time commitment.

What Makes a Good Book Cover

A good book cover is more than just decoration. It's a critical marketing tool that influences whether a reader will stop scrolling, pick up the book or click to learn more. A professionally designed cover doesn't just look appealing; it also sends a message about the book's genre, tone and quality. It should evoke the right emotional response, set expectations and speak clearly to its intended audience.

What follows is information on what makes a book cover effective and why investing in professional design is essential—especially in a saturated market.

The Cover's Purpose: Signal, Sell, Suggest

A book cover serves three main purposes:

- **Signal the genre**—Within a glance, the reader should know whether your book is a romance, thriller, fantasy, memoir or literary novel. Design elements such as typography, colour palette and imagery all work together to establish the category.

- **Sell the book**—A great cover grabs attention and compels interest. It should hold its own in a crowded online marketplace and make readers want to click on the book or turn it over in a store.

- **Suggest the tone and content**—A cover should offer a taste of the story or mood inside. A gothic thriller and a light-hearted romantic comedy may both feature a house on the front—but the styling should immediately differentiate them.

If a cover fails to meet these three objectives, it can create confusion or mislead readers, ultimately impacting reviews and sales.

Genre Expectations Matter

Each genre has visual conventions that signal to readers: *This book is for you*. Deviating too far from genre norms can result in a cover that looks beautiful but confuses or repels the intended audience.

For example:

- **Fantasy** often features ornate fonts, moody lighting, and mystical or medieval elements.
- **Romance** may include character-driven imagery, warmer tones and soft light.
- **Thrillers** favour stark contrasts, bold fonts and dynamic visual tension.
- **Memoir** covers often focus on a single powerful image, sometimes of the author themselves, with clean type.

A good designer will research current bestsellers in your genre to align your cover with reader expectations while still making it unique.

Typography: Clarity and Hierarchy

Your title needs to be **legible at thumbnail size**— especially for online listings. Decorative or script fonts can be effective in the right context, but readability should always come first. The same goes for your name and any subtitle.

Typography should also reflect the tone of the book:

- Serif fonts = classic, serious, traditional
- Sans-serif = modern, clean, informal
- Handwritten = personal, whimsical, emotional

A skilled designer will establish visual hierarchy, ensuring the most important text elements are the most eye-catching.

Colour and Emotion

Colours evoke emotion and can suggest genre and mood. Cool colours (blue, green, grey) often convey calm, mystery or professionalism. Warm colours (red, orange, pink) can suggest passion, energy or tension.

Contrast helps text stand out. High-contrast designs are more eye-catching, while muted or monochrome palettes can suggest subtlety or literary quality.

Good designers don't just pick colours they like—they use them intentionally to support the book's identity and market positioning.

Imagery and Symbolism

Cover imagery can be literal (a scene or object from the book) or symbolic (a metaphor or motif that represents the theme). The key is that it must:

- be visually striking
- reproduce well in both colour and greyscale
- not be misleading

Too much detail can overwhelm the viewer. One strong image is more powerful than many small ones. Good designers use imagery to reinforce the emotional impact of the book and make it memorable.

Don't expect or ask the designer to load the cover with something to represent every aspect of the book. The cover shouldn't tell the whole story; rather, it should hint at it with imagery that stimulates the reader's imagination.

Simplicity Wins

Crowded covers are hard to read, especially on digital platforms. The best covers often follow the 'one strong idea' rule. This might be:
- one clear image
- one dominant colour
- one typeface (with variations)

Simplicity also helps reinforce branding. Think of iconic covers—*The Great Gatsby*, *Twilight* or *The Girl with the Dragon Tattoo*. Each has a bold, simple concept that lodges in the memory.

Professional Design vs Do it Yourself

Many authors are tempted to design their own covers. Unless you have professional training in graphic design and understand market dynamics, this is rarely a good idea. DIY covers often:
- are poorly balanced
- use inappropriate fonts
- confuse genre signals
- are visually cluttered or bland

A professionally designed cover signals quality to

the reader and to the industry. It shows that you value your work—and encourages others to take it seriously too.

If you're self-publishing and working with a designer, make sure to:

- give a short, clear design brief (genre, tone, core ideas)
- provide comparable covers you like (and explain why)
- be open to expert suggestions
- avoid micromanaging

If you're traditionally published, you likely won't have much say in your cover design. But you can provide input when invited—and remember, the publisher is aiming to sell the book just like you are. Their design choices are rooted in market experience.

Series Branding

If you're writing a series, it's essential that each book's cover looks related—using consistent fonts, layout and design style. This builds brand recognition and helps readers identify books that belong together.

A good designer will establish a series look

from the start, so future books can be updated easily while maintaining a unified aesthetic.

Title vs Cover Concept

Sometimes, a clever title and a clever cover don't play well together. One should do the heavy lifting, while the other supports. If your title is abstract or literary, your cover might need to be more literal to give clarity. If your title is very descriptive, your cover can afford to be more symbolic or subtle.

A Silent Salesperson

Your book cover is your potential reader's first impression. It's not just a visual—it's a silent salesperson. It must speak directly to your audience and compel them to take the next step.

Invest in professional design. Trust your publisher or designer's genre knowledge. And remember that a good book cover isn't about expressing your personal taste—it's about connecting with your readers.

The right cover will not only attract attention— it will set the tone for the entire reading experience.

Working with a Book Cover Designer

When an author lands a deal with a mainstream publisher, one of the first surprises they encounter is their lack of control over their book cover design. While this might seem disheartening, there's a solid rationale behind it. Just as authors need editors to refine their narratives, they need professional designers to craft compelling covers.

Authors are intimately connected to their stories, and that can cloud their judgement when it comes to cover design. They often envision covers that encapsulate every detailed element of their narrative. However, a cover's primary role is to sell the book, not to summarise it. A cluttered cover can confuse potential readers, while a well-designed one piques curiosity and invites exploration.

This chapter is for those who do have some say

in their cover and want to get the best out of their cover designer.

The Publisher's Perspective: Selling the Story

Publishers and designers focus on creating covers that resonate with the target audience. They aim to convey the genre and mood of the book, often opting for subtlety over explicit detail. A cover that leaves some mystery encourages readers to delve deeper, sparking interest and engagement.

A successful book cover often raises questions rather than providing answers. It should make readers do a double-take, offering just enough intrigue to prompt them to pick up the book or click on its thumbnail. A cover that stands out in a crowded market is one that balances genre conventions with a unique twist.

The Role of the Author: Collaborator, Not Controller

You, as the author, should view yourself as a collaborator in the cover design process. While it's beneficial to share ideas about the book's mood or significant symbols, it's crucial to allow designers the creative freedom to interpret these elements. The designer will create the most effective cover if you give your ideas at the start of the process and then let the designer work. Authors who rigidly adhere to their preconceived notions and start asking for endless rounds of revisions often end up with less effective covers.

At Alkira Publishing, the cover design process is a collaborative effort involving the publisher, managing editor and designer. This ensures that the cover aligns with the book's essence while appealing to its intended audience. Authors are encouraged to provide feedback but should ultimately trust the expertise of the professionals involved.

Embracing the Expertise

Book cover design is a specialised art form that requires a keen understanding of market trends and reader psychology. You should embrace the expertise of your publishers and designers, trusting them to create covers that captivate and sell. You'll get the best cover by stepping back and allowing professionals to work their magic.

Understanding the nuances of book cover design can be challenging, but it's essential for the success of your work. By recognising the value of professional input and embracing the collaborative process, you can achieve a cover that not only reflects your story but also captivates your audience.

PART SEVEN:
BOOK PROMOTION

Book Promotion Myths

If you're like most writers, you'd rather be writing than promoting. You've poured your heart into your book, maybe even revised it ten times, and now all you want is for someone else—anyone else—to do the rest. That's understandable. I feel the same way, and I wish it could happen that way, but when it comes to book promotion, there are a few myths floating around that can lead you astray, especially if you're just starting out.

Let's bust some of those myths before they trip you up.

Myth 1: 'If I Get a Mainstream Publisher, They'll Do All the Promotion for Me.'

Oh, if only. This is the big one. So many aspiring authors think that landing a traditional publishing deal means the publisher will roll out the red carpet and shout about your book from every rooftop.

The truth? Unless you're a celebrity or they've given you a six-figure advance, you'll be doing most of the promotion yourself. You might get a spot in a seasonal catalogue, maybe a few copies sent out for review, but that won't be enough to make your book visible amongst the flood of new releases.

Publishers focus their marketing dollars where they believe they'll get the biggest return—and that's rarely on debut or midlist authors. If you want your book to succeed, you need to be prepared to talk about it, share it and show up for it.

They [mainstream publishers] just wait and see how the market responds. They're going to wait and see if it gains traction somehow on its own, maybe by luck or because of the author's efforts. If it gains traction, they'll start putting money behind it, but that is no way to market.

If you're an author with one of the Big Five traditional publishers that are using this strategy, that means they will spend zero money on your book, and your book launch is all on you.

If you do your homework and have a good launch, and your book is "doing numbers" suddenly, marketing money becomes available. But if your book is not doing well, no marketing money is made available.[10]

Myth 2: 'I'll Hire a Marketing Firm, and They'll Make My Book a Bestseller.'

This one's tempting, isn't it? You don't want to be pushy, or you don't know where to start, so you figure paying someone else to do it is the answer.

But marketing isn't magic. No one—no matter how slick their pitch—is going to care about your book the way you do. And no one can guarantee sales. Most marketing firms will do things like run Amazon ads, create social posts and maybe get you some reviews. That can help—but only if your book is well written, well-packaged and hits the

---

10. https://www.authormedia.com/publishing-industry-secrets-revealed-at-the-penguin-random-house-trial

right audience.

Spending thousands of dollars won't fix a vague blurb, a poorly chosen title or a cover that doesn't match your genre. And it won't substitute for authentic connection with readers. Readers can tell when you care, and that matters more than any automated ad campaign.

Myth 3: 'If the Book Is Good, It Will Sell Itself.'

This one's so persistent, it feels like it should be true. Great book = great sales, right?

Unfortunately, good writing isn't enough. There are brilliant books out there languishing in obscurity simply because no one knows they exist. If you don't make some noise about your book, no one will find it.

That doesn't mean you have to be loud, extroverted or salesy. But it does mean you have to be visible. Find a way that suits your personality— it may be writing thoughtful blog posts, creating beautiful Bookstagram photos or chatting on podcasts. You don't need to do everything, but you do need to do something.

Myth 4: 'Social Media Is the Only Way to Sell Books.'

It's easy to think that if you're not dancing on TikTok or tweeting ten times a day, you're doomed.

The truth? Social media is just one tool in the toolbox. It works better for some genres than others, but only if you use it in a way that's authentic to you. Some authors do brilliantly on YouTube or Instagram. Others focus on newsletters, podcast interviews or local events.

You don't have to do everything. Choose a few things you can do consistently and well.

Myth 5: 'Once the Book's Out, the Hard Part Is Over.'

Ah, this one stings a bit. After months (or years) of writing and revising, getting the cover right, formatting, proofreading—you finally hit 'publish' or your book lands on shelves.

But launch day is just the beginning. Book promotion is a long game. Your book needs consistent, ongoing support. Not full-time, not forever—but enough that it doesn't sink beneath the waves.

Set up a sustainable rhythm: maybe one post a

week, one interview a month, one local bookstore event per quarter. Keep showing up for your book, even after the excitement fades.

Myth 6: 'I'm Not the Kind of Person Who Can Promote a Book.'

If you've ever thought, 'I'm too introverted. I don't have time. I don't know how'—you're not alone. But promoting your book doesn't have to mean turning into someone you're not.

There's no one right way to promote. You can build relationships one reader at a time. You can write articles or start a quiet newsletter. You can collaborate with others or work solo. The key is to find an approach that feels manageable and real.

You've already done the hard part—writing the book. Now it's just about letting people know it's there in a way that fits who you are.

Bottom Line

Book promotion doesn't require shouting, selling your soul or outsourcing your voice. It just needs you—consistent, creative and present—to turn up places where you and your book can be found. Do what you can to get those initial sales, but the important thing is to focus on setting up a long-term strategy that you can maintain. With print on demand, your book will be available until you unpublish it, so sales can continue for decades. If you want to sell books in any kind of ongoing fashion, then be prepared for the long game. Choose things you enjoy doing and stick with them.

Your Author Platform

An author platform is your web base—essentially your website and social media presence—and you need to start getting it set up well before publication. Social media should be set up as soon as you start writing, because it can take years to build a social media following. The longer the time you give yourself, the less stress you'll have when you discover that it takes a while to get followers.

But setting up a web presence isn't just a matter of making a website and getting some social media happening, because there's no point doing any of that until you have a brand to promote and an idea of who your ideal reader is. You need to know who you're looking to connect with and how you're going to present yourself and your book.

Important note: Your author brand is you, not your book. That's probably not something you want to hear if you're someone who doesn't like the idea of promoting yourself. You probably think that you can promote the book and not yourself—and that's okay if you're only ever going to publish one book, but do you want to limit yourself that way? You can only talk about a book so much before people turn off, but you can share your passions and interests for a lot longer—and relate them to your book for the purpose of promotion. Everything you write is an expression of you, and you are the thing that connects them all together.

What follows in this chapter are the essentials of marketing, and though the specific ways you can promote might change, these basic steps never do. If you don't know what you're selling and to whom you're selling, you can't sell, so don't skip attending to these basic considerations. Do more reading on each point to get the full picture. The internet has plenty of resources for book marketing—just don't get caught by adverts offering big promotional results for no or little effort on your part, apart from what you'll pay them. No one can guarantee book sales, and if they say they can, it's probably a scam.

Make a Profile of Your Ideal Reader

- Who would like your book? Be specific with age, sex, interests.
- What might they be looking for that your book would provide?
- What will they get out of your book?
- Draw up reader profiles. Give them names so you can remember them when you write blog or social media posts, so you can talk directly to them.
- List where your personal story will connect with these readers. Are they parents like you, for example? Or have you both experienced the death of a partner?

Decide on Your Brand as an Author.

What and why are you writing? And what are you going to project to the world in your role as an author that will help you connect with your ideal reader? (This will develop as time passes, so don't feel you have to 'get it right' first time.)

- Come up with a mission statement for your writing (what and why you write).
- Come up with a tagline that encapsulates your writing. For example, 'Writing that is not

afraid of the dark.'

- What mood do you want to give people who visit your website or follow you on social media?
- Choose colours and images that reflect your brand/mood. Select around ten images to use on your website and social media profiles that look like they belong together. If you're unsure, choose colours and images that relate to your book cover. Good free images can be found on sites like Pixabay. You can also ask your cover designer if you can use the source images they used to create your cover, or you can use AI to create your own images.
- Get a quality photo taken of you in a setting and in clothing that relates to your brand.
- Choose one photo to be your main photo on your website and Facebook page and one to be your profile picture. These should be the same across all accounts. Your picture makes the best profile picture. People relate better to someone whose face they can see.
- Write an author's bio that reflects your branding—see the next chapter.

Set up Socia Media Accounts

Set up a Facebook account and connect with people you know who are already on Facebook. Facebook makes this easy for you. You can connect with people you already know on this account—those you agree to add as 'friends'—but you can also use your privacy settings to allow people you don't know to follow you. When someone follows you, they can see your public posts in their News Feed, even if they are not your friend. You can manage who can follow you by adjusting your 'Followers and Public Content' settings.

The usual advice is to also set up a Facebook business page with your author name (not book name). Facebook pages are designed for businesses, and setting one up is more complex than just opening a personal account. A page allows you to separate your author self from your private self. People can follow you as an author rather than as a private individual. However, it's difficult to get followers to a page, and unless you pay Facebook to boost your posts, few of those followers will ever see them.

If you have no intention of giving any money to Facebook, don't intend any personal use of Facebook and don't want to be posting on a page as well as your personal profile, then a page may not be best for you. But if you use just your personal account, you can't boost your posts or take out Facebook adverts.

Whether you decide to have a page or just a personal account, be yourself, be genuine and aim to connect with your ideal reader. If you're new to social media, you'll also need to do some research on how the algorithms work and how to get engagement on your posts.

It's best to start with just one social media account, and Facebook is a good place to begin. If your readers are young adults, though, it would be better to focus on Instagram. Look at the different options and choose whichever site or sites resonate most with you and your ideal reader. Set up any further social media accounts that interest you, and join Facebook groups that relate to your book's themes.

Some authors are reticent to bite the social media bullet, but you can use it entirely for your writing business and not get caught up in the social media jungle. At the very least, you can have an account and support your publisher—if you have one—to promote your book by liking, commenting on and sharing their posts about your book.

Set up an Email List

Email lists are recommended for authors, because they are a guaranteed way to get your message out to those on your list. On social media, you rely on the algorithm to put your posts before your followers, and the reality is that most will never see them. However, an email will get to their inbox. It doesn't mean they will open or read it, but at least it gets to where they can see it. Having an email list is vital if you're planning more than one book.

Use an email list client like MailerLite with proper ways for readers to sign up and unsubscribe if they want. Don't use lists in your Gmail or Hotmail and so on, as legally you need a way for people to unsubscribe. Also, don't add people to your list without their permission.

Once you have a signup link for your email list, you can share it on your social media accounts. Try to offer something free to encourage people to sign up. A short story, perhaps, or a checklist that relates to a topic you touch on in your book.

Set up a Website with Pages and Potential for a Blog

The best way to go about setting up a website is to do it yourself, not just because it's cheapest, but also because it's not as difficult as you might think. When you do it yourself, making changes and adding blog posts is simple. You really don't want to have to pay someone every time you want to change something.

- Start with a free wordpress.com site and your own URL with your name.com or name_author.com.
- Choose a template that fits with the colours and style you chose for your branding. Have a photo on every page.
- Make pages titled About (bio & mission statement), Books, Blog, Contact.
- Set up the sharing function so posts automatically share to your Facebook page (and any other social media accounts you have).
- Make sure you have a widget that enables readers to sign up for your email list to get notifications of new blog posts, and ones that allow them to follow you on your social media accounts.

Start a Blog

You don't have to have a blog. But then you don't *have* to have any of this, either. Some people say that blogs are dead, but the fact remains that a blog on your own website is the only place where your writing can't be taken down by someone else. You can set your blog posts to automatically go out on your email list direct to your readers.

Wordpress provides an option for people to sign up to follow your blog, but it's better to set up your own email list and use that one. With your own email list, you ensure that your blog posts end up in people's inboxes.

The idea is that you use your blog content as your reader-connection topic for a month and take excerpts from those posts for your social media posts. Links on social media send people back to your website to read the full blog post, and there they find your book.

- Make a list of topics for blogs that speak to your ideal reader, things that relate to your book's content or themes. You can also share any aspect of your life and passions that your ideal reader might be interested in or that builds on your points of connection.
- Write a postscript for your blog posts that

directs readers to your book, social media accounts and email signup.

- Aim to write a post of at least 500–800 words every week on one of the topics your ideal reader would enjoy. Start with every fortnight or every month if you prefer, but be regular and keep it going. Even if you have few readers— you have to start somewhere. A platform is a starting point, and it builds over time.
- Even if you're not getting many readers, keep at it, because regularly updating your site with a blog post makes your website more favourable for search engines.
- Always include a photo in the post. Be yourself. Research 'How to write a good blog post' for inspiration.
- To build your readership, find other blogs and Facebook groups on topics in which your ideal reader might be interested. Visit them and read and make intelligent comments on those blogs. People may then come to your blog and follow you. Don't try to sell your book; just be yourself and say what you feel. Be genuine, and people will become interested in you. Hard sells do not work. Being a nice person with intelligent or wise opinions does work. It's all about building a relationship with people.

- Use your blog to announce progress on your book and, of course, its publication and purchase outlets. Also, use it to ask for people willing to read and review your book on Amazon.

These are the key elements of an author platform from which you can launch your book. Don't expect it to have lots of visitors straight away; be in it for the long haul and set a schedule you can sustain.

Write an Author's Bio That Reflects Your Branding

Writing your author bio can feel more awkward than writing a first kiss scene. You're supposed to capture your identity, your tone and your professional credentials in just a few sentences. You want to sound confident but not boastful, friendly but not too casual, interesting but not try-hard.

It's a lot to ask of a paragraph. But it's important, because your bio isn't just about listing your accomplishments—it's about communicating your brand as an author. And if your brand is unclear or inconsistent, it's harder for readers to connect with you and know what to expect from your work.

Before you write a word, take a moment to think about your author brand. Your brand isn't your logo or font—it's the feeling readers associate with you and your work. Are you insightful and lyrical? Playful and bold? Practical and empowering?

If you're not sure, look at your writing voice. Look at your themes. Look at what readers say about your stories. Your author bio should be in alignment with that tone.

You don't need to say *everything*—you just need to say what's *true* and *relevant*. If you're writing magical realism with metaphysical themes, your bio should hint at the same depth and sense of wonder. If your stories are fast-paced thrillers, your bio should feel sharp and dynamic. The language you use in your bio should *sound* like you.

Tips for Writing Your Bio

Choose Your Tone to Match Your Books

Write in the same voice you write your books in. If your novel is introspective and poetic, a jokey bio will feel jarring. If your writing is quirky or humorous, then let that humour shine.

Write in Third Person (Unless on Your Website)

For books and product pages, stick to third person. That's the industry standard. But on your website, where you can be more conversational, writing in first person can help readers feel more connected.

Include Your Genre and Themes

Readers (and algorithms) need to know what kind of books you write. Include the genre, and if your work explores certain themes—like neurodivergence, self-discovery or mythological worlds—mention that too.

Mention Relevant Credentials or Experience

Only include qualifications or experience that relate to your writing. A degree in astrophysics might be relevant if you write hard sci-fi. Years working as a psychologist? Great for psychological thrillers or introspective fiction.

If you don't have formal credentials, don't worry—your lived experience is valid. You can frame it like:

'She draws on her background in art and spiritual practice to create layered stories of transformation and inner journeying.'

Include One Personal Detail

This helps readers remember you. Keep it short and true to you. Example:
'She lives on the south coast of NSW, Australia, and decorates forest-themed hats in her spare time.'

End With a Link or Call to Action (If Space Allows)

On a website or longer bio, you might say something like:
'You can find her animated art stories on her YouTube channel, Tahlia Dreaming, or explore her art and craft at tahliasartandcraft.au.'

In General

Your author bio is not a résumé. It's a little window into your world—a taste of your voice, your values and your creative identity. You can write different versions for different uses but keep them all aligned with your brand so that wherever your reader finds you, they'll feel the same tone and energy that lives in your books.

You don't have to impress everyone. You just have to *be yourself.* That's what branding is—clarity, consistency and connection.

Finding Reviewers to Write Reviews on Amazon

Reviews are important social proof for readers. Good reviews—and even bad ones—help readers to know if they will enjoy your work. I mentioned getting professional editorial reviews for your back cover, but they won't show up on your product page since you have paid for them. Reader reviews are what's needed for your Amazon page, but getting them takes some effort.

Readers will not review your book unless you ask them, so when you add the front and back matter to your manuscript before formatting, make sure your book includes a request at the end of the book for readers to leave a review at their point of purchase. You'll also need to get reviews from people who have not yet read your book, and you will need to give them a free copy.

Aim to get around 25–50 reviews on your Amazon page—that number makes readers feel that the reviews give a good indication of the quality and likability of the book. Make sure you only ask people who are likely to enjoy your book; remember your ideal reader? Start with friends and family, but only if they read the kind of book that you've written.

Find people to review your book through:

- Blog listings – such as http://www.theindieview. com/indie-reviewers/. These people are often booked up way in advance, so it can be months before you get a review. It can be quite difficult these days to get answers from bloggers, but it will only cost you your time.
- Blog tour companies. Ask for recommendations in author groups.
- Some companies that sell advertising also have a service where they will arrange to find reviewers for you for a fee, but make sure you aren't paying the actual reviewers for positive reviews, as that is unethical and against Amazon policy. Ask in author groups for recommendations and always check by internet searching the name of the service along with the word 'scam'. The

number of reviews can easily fall short of what you expect, but it is easier than trying to find people yourself. Booksirens and Booksprout are often mentioned as worthwhile.

Book Launches

There are basically two ways to run a book launch—online and in person. A successful book launch does both, but not necessarily at the same time.

Online Book Launch

An online book launch includes things like:
- A series of blog posts and emails to your email list over a period of six weeks before the publication date, ending with an 'Out Now' blog post. This is to build anticipation. Each post should reveal more about the book—coming soon, cover reveal, pre-order now and 'Out Now' posts.
- The same postings for social media accounts using good graphics that stand out.
- Arrange for people to leave reviews on the book

page as soon as it goes live. This is vital even if you do nothing else.

- Book a blog tour to get your book seen. Blog tours don't usually directly generate sales, but they can get reviews (not necessarily good ones) and they do expose readers to the book. They may buy it later when they see it on a promo, for instance.
- Consider a 99c sale for release day to get new readers and get your book higher up the Amazon rankings. The higher it is, the more people will see it. Such a sale needs to be advertised through one of the many sites that advertise reduced-price books.
- A cross-promotion with other authors—they share your offer or new release post with their email list and social media accounts, and you share their offers with yours.

In-Person Book Launch

- Set a budget. Keep it small unless you know you'll get a hundred people to the launch.
- Choose a venue. Our local authors often use the Kiama Library because it's free and they have an email list to which they advertise the book launch.

- Contact local newspapers, radio and TV stations. Send them a media kit and a reason to do an article or interview on you and your book.
- Tell your friends about it. Send an email to your author email list.
- Contact local organisations whose members might be interested in it and ask for a little space in their newsletter to advertise it.
- Arrange catering if you want to include drinks and nibbles in the event. This is not necessary but is a nice touch where possible and practical. It depends on the venue, the kind of book, the time of day, and most importantly, your budget.
- Find someone to introduce you and any guest speakers, and to ask you questions about the book.
- If your publisher or editor is local, then ask one of them to speak about the book.
- Plan an audio-visual presentation if you can. It may be showing your book trailer, or photos of the setting, or photos that inspired the characters.
- Choose a short passage to read—around 800 words. If you don't have a good reading voice and aren't comfortable speaking in public, then ask someone with a good reading voice to do

it for you.
- Arrange the running order for the day.
- Do it once in one venue, and if you can, do it again in another venue in another town. Perhaps as part of a meeting of a social group whose interests align with the content of the book.

Of course, the more friends you have and the more organisations you belong to, the greater your chance of having a successful in-person book launch. And if you have it videoed and edited down into short snippets, you can also use it on social media and your blog as one way to keep the momentum going after the launch.

Do You Need a Media Kit?

A media kit is what an author or publisher gives to anyone they contact asking them to help promote their book. It includes information about the author and the book as well as a press release that captures their attention. Interview questions and an excerpt, along with a list of awards, other books written and information about upcoming events like a book launch, can also be included.

A media kit is usually in a PDF format that can be emailed to media contacts or printed out for distribution by mail or in person.

When Do Authors Need a Media Kit?

If you're planning to contact bloggers or traditional media (newspapers, magazines, radio, television) about your book's publication, you'll need a media kit that includes a press release and suggested interview questions. A printed version of this is useful if you intend to give talks somewhere you can't sell your books directly (or may run out of copies). They are also handy to take to local bookstores to encourage them to stock your book.

A well-written press release not only makes the recipient want to talk about the book, it also makes it easy for them to do exactly that. They can copy and paste something interesting into their blog or paper without having to write it themselves. A list of questions makes an interview with the author more appealing because they don't have to think up appropriate questions themselves. If you contact a reviewer and they can't manage to commit to reading and reviewing your book, they can still pop something about it into their blog simply by taking something from your media kit.

What's in a Media Kit?

It's important that a media kit be well designed so it gives a professional impression. Apart from the words, the graphic design must look good and reflect your book. A media kit could have some or all of the following in it:

- a cover page
- your brief author bio and a photo
- a quote from the author relevant to the book
- your contact details—where and how you want them to contact you
- your social media accounts
- your book blurb, book details (number of pages, formats, ISBNs, publisher name, etc.), cover image, and two to four really good reviews
- where people can buy the book
- a brief, exciting excerpt—no more than one page
- a little bit about other books you've written and their covers
- details of upcoming events
- a list of awards
- notable media appearances
- interview questions and answers that delve into what's interesting in your book
- press release—why it's newsworthy. Write

something they can copy and paste into their paper.

A good excerpt for a media kit should be concise and impactful, typically around 500–1000 words. The excerpt should be a standalone piece that effectively showcases the author's writing style and the book's themes without requiring extensive context.

You could wade your way through the many free press-release templates on Canva to try to find a design you can adapt, but I didn't find much there that was directly relevant for authors. I did find templates useful for authors on Etsy, however. You'll have to pay for one, but you can use it for all your books. If you don't want to have to play around with graphic design tools yourself, you can give the information to your cover designer and ask them to design it for you.

How to Write a Press Release

Media outlets will not be interested in your book just because it's a new book out. It must have some angle that makes it newsworthy. A successful press release will make them interested enough to get back to you. Ask yourself: What is it about your book that makes it news? What angle can you take on it that would make a paper want to write about it? Here are some ideas:

- a unique or fascinating book topic
- a shocking or captivating author story
- a rare or prestigious book award won
- an impressive or intimidating milestone
- an unconventional promotional effort
- an endorsement or link to something/someone famous
- tying in your book with a 'buzz' concept, e.g., millennials, gluten free or any other 'hot topic' that a journalist will see and think, *Yeah, people will click that.*

A Standalone Press Release Should Include the Following:

- attention-grabbing headline of fewer than twenty words
- your city/state/country and date
- intro—a unique or interesting angle, problem/solution hook
- author quotation—something strong
- *mini* author bio—one small paragraph
- book description—around 180 words
- contact details—links to your website, email, phone number (for local media), social media

and how to get review copies
- call to action—ask for what you want
- traditionally, they end with the hash symbol, three times, centred

When the Press Release Is Part of a Media Kit

Only the following is required, because the rest of it is elsewhere in the media kit:
- attention-grabbing headline of fewer than twenty words
- intro—a unique or interesting angle, problem/solution hook
- a one- or two-sentence description of the book
- an author quotation—perhaps your mission statement as an author
- call to action—for example, ask for an interview or a review

Social Media Book Launch Plan

Here is a social media plan you could use to launch a new book on Instagram, Facebook and other social media platforms:

- **Build anticipation on social media**: Start by creating a buzz about the upcoming book launch on all social media platforms. Share teasers, behind-the-scenes images and snippets from the book. Use hashtags related to the book, and encourage your followers to share the posts with their friends.

- **Create a launch event**: Host a launch party or book signing event and promote it on social media. Share images and videos of the event on Instagram, Facebook and X/Twitter. Encourage attendees to share their experiences on social media by creating a custom hashtag.

- **Share sneak peeks of the book**: Share sneak peeks of the book, such as the cover design, chapter titles and quotes from the book. Use visually appealing images to grab the attention of your followers.
- **Host a giveaway**: Host a giveaway on social media to promote the book launch. Encourage followers to share the post and tag their friends to enter the giveaway. The prize could be a signed copy of the book, a merchandise pack or a free consultation with the author.
- **Collaborate with influencers**: Collaborate with influencers in your niche to promote the book launch. Reach out to influencers on Instagram, X/Twitter, LinkedIn and Facebook who have a large following and are interested in books. Offer them a free copy of the book in exchange for a review or a social media post.
- **Share reviews and testimonials**: Share positive reviews and testimonials from readers who have read the book. Use their quotes to create visually appealing images to share on social media. Encourage followers to share their own reviews using the book's hashtag.
- **Use paid advertising:** Use paid advertising on social media platforms to reach a wider audience. Create targeted ads based on

audience demographics and interests. Use visually appealing images and compelling copy to grab the attention of potential readers.

By following these steps, you can create a social media plan to launch a new book on social media. Remember, however, that only a small percentage of your followers will see these posts, and fewer will buy your book. I say this not to depress you, but to help you have realistic expectations. Even so, these are the steps to follow, no matter how small your accounts, and if you have a small but engaged following, you can do better than someone with a large following where the followers have no relationship with the author. Building relationships is the key to social media.

Some Promotion Options for Ebooks

Most indie authors run occasional cut-price promotions (one every three to six months or so) to raise awareness of their book and give sales a boost. To do the following, you need to have published your ebook on your own account so that you have direct control over the pricing:

- Reduce your book to 99c and advertise the sale.
- The best places to advertise are those with email lists that target specific reader interests; for example, Freebooksy, Bargain Booksy, Kindle Nation Daily, Book Gorilla, Ereader News Today, Pixel of Ink, Bookbub and so on.
- If you set your ebook up on KDP and list it in Kindle Select, it will appear in the Kindle Unlimited library, where members of the library can read it for free. You can list your book free

for five days in a ninety-day period. You can also do a seven-day cut-price promotion and still get a 70% royalty on sales—normally you only get 35% if you list your book below $2.99. If you do this, you can ask reviewers to pick up the book during those five free days. You need to advertise the sale though (as above), because the idea is to sell lots of books to push your book up the Amazon rankings.

- Another advantage of setting your ebook up on KDP is that you can set up Amazon adverts. There are free courses where you can learn to do this, or you can pay others to do it for you. From an economic point of view, learning to do it yourself is going to be a far better return on your investment, but getting someone to do it for you is worth a try if you don't feel confident doing it yourself. Paying the book promotion service for their time and expertise increases the cost of adverts considerably, however, so be prepared to lose money on the adverts. By doing them yourself, you should at least break even.

- Facebook adverts: Good for getting people to sign up for your newsletter if you have a giveaway, not so good for selling books directly.

The Long-Term View of Book Promotion

The best way to sell more books is to write more books so you have many books available for sale. When a reader enjoys one of your books, they will likely want to read all the rest. So any promotions and advertising you do on one book can lead to sales of your other books. Also, you can't keep talking about the same book over and over—people will tune out—but you can talk about new ones!

If you're planning a series or intending to write several books, it's a good idea to start an email list of fans somewhere like MailerLite, so you can talk to them via their inbox. Email list building is a specialised area, but you can research 'How to Build an Email list'. Services like BookFunnel are designed to assist in this process.

Keep posting on your blog, keep building

connections with people on social media and keep having promos. Advertise your promos in several places over the period of the promotion.

Your book may be excellent, but it will only sell in large numbers if it appeals to large numbers of people *and* if you can reach those people to tell them about it. You have a lot of competition.

Always research companies you're thinking of spending marketing money with (Google their name and the word 'scam' to check out that aspect), and ask in your author support groups if anyone has any experience with the company.

How Do You Define Success?

Few authors achieve bestselling status or make a living just from their writing. Many manage with a part-time job to add to their income, but most authors will never be in a situation to give up their day job. That's fine if you're not trying to be a full-time author. And why should you?

If you're a full-time author, you must keep producing books whether you're inspired or not. For me, that pressure would be a problem. Someone who's not aiming to be a career author isn't necessarily any less serious about their writing than someone who is, but they'll have different goals, expectations and definitions of success.

I expect a lot of authors don't achieve the kind of success they crave because most fail to get published by a selective publisher. Rejection notices are the norm, and I've previously given you the statistics for book sales for both mainstream and indie publishers. I'm not trying to depress you, just giving a healthy dose of reality. Unrealistic expectations lead to feelings of failure.

Success in Terms of Book Sales

If you define success in terms of book sales, how many books exactly do you need to sell to be a success? How do you choose a realistic number? Or do you just leave it loosely defined as 'bestseller' or 'hundreds of books' or 'thousands of books'?

You might be the author who hits the big time. Who knows? But there is no guarantee that anyone will even like your book. All you can do is write what you're passionate about, find a good editor to help you, and do your best to get a good publisher and make some sales. The rest is up to the universe.

Sales depend on fashions and luck as much as quality and promotional skill. Books have always sold through word of mouth, and it's still the same. People talking about your book is what will sell it, but whether people chat to their friends about a book is a nebulous element over which we have no control. It might happen. It might not. And if we define success as something that might not happen through no fault of our own, then we're likely to end up feeling like a failure. And no one wants to feel like a failure.

The trouble with defining your success in terms of book sales is that you have a very limited criterion on which to evaluate your success and limited control over how it plays out. If you fail to make 'big' sales, it's not necessarily—and likely not—your fault. Luckily, a successful book can be measured by much more than sales.

Success in Terms of Your Goals

In the chapter titled 'Which Publishing Option is Best for You', we looked at your goals for writing and publishing a book, and when you come to evaluating the success of your project, this is where you need to look. Regardless of sales, the real marker of success is how well your book did in terms of your goals.

If you want a literary career, then any step towards that is a success. It's extremely unlikely that you will get that mainstream deal first time around, but you wrote a good book—and you know it's good because of reviews and maybe an award—and you learned a lot, so the next time it will all go more smoothly. If your goal was simply to hold your published book in your hand, be proud of it, and have your family and friends read and enjoy it, then that's what success looks like for you. Don't be seduced into taking sales as your marker of success.

When I wrote my first book, I set my marker of success as writing and publishing a quality book, and when I got awards and good reviews, I took that as success. Of course, part of me longed for great sales and to be the talk of the town—all authors harbour that dream—but I wasn't surprised or disappointed when that didn't happen. I decided on self-publishing—which is how I learned to publish others—though I didn't cover my costs. Breaking even financially was another success, but I had to wait several years and write several more books for that to happen.

The effort I had to put into promoting my books to get that success, however, was too much for me. Now, I consider any new book of mine a success if I manage to get it published in among all the editing and publishing I do for others. I don't do big promotional pushes or spend a lot of money on a book launch; they just quietly add to my stock of books and sell slowly over time. With this simple aim, I can't fail. Financially, I have no expectations of any book covering its costs, but my costs are relatively low, and my editing and publishing work covers any shortfall. Like my art, my writing is a hobby, and my advice to anyone writing a book is that, unless you are prepared to operate your writing as a business with all that entails, then it's best you treat it the same way as you would any hobby.

As an author, you could earn big, or you could earn very little—or something in between. Your book might get a lot of good reviews, or it might get enough bad ones to seriously affect sales. You may be a long way from covering costs, or you may get them all back within a couple of years. Somewhere between those sliding scales lies success or failure, depending on how you define success. So ask yourself: 'How do I define success?'

Final Words

Congratulations on reaching the end of this guide. You now know how to go from the first spark of inspiration all the way through to publishing and promoting your book. You can choose to do all of it, none of it or some of it.

I hope I have given you the technical grounding to:

- write with confidence
- evaluate and improve your work
- find a team who can help you turn your book into a professional product
- have some understanding of the basics of book promotion

Hopefully, you have also gained some emotional support to help you weather the common challenges authors meet when writing a novel and bringing it to publication.

Writing a book is a significant investment of time, effort and money, but if you do it for yourself—rather than for riches or fame—you cannot fail. Authors get great satisfaction from bringing their visions to life, and when our writing comes from the heart and is professionally finished, the completed product is a worthy addition to the body of human literature. This is true not because all our novels are equally brilliant, but because every story written in an author's unique voice has value. Stories are the lifeblood of human culture.

The writing journey is not just about learning how to write and publish a book; it's also a psychological and spiritual journey. True inspiration comes from the groundless space of potentiality within us. It's the space that opens up in times of quiet reflection, prayer or meditation, and seeing such inspiration through from its initial spark to its published state is a worthy thing for us to do, regardless of the outcome.

Do not let the potential downsides of the writing journey keep you from fulfilling your writing dream. Write that book. Enjoy doing it. See any frustrations and setbacks as part of the joy of it. Approach it with gusto, and feel a wonderful sense of accomplishment when you finally hold that book in your hand.

Good writing and good luck!

A Note from the Author

If you enjoyed this book, I would be very grateful if you could write a review and publish it at your point of purchase. Your review, even a brief one, will help other readers to decide whether they'll enjoy my work.

If you want to be notified of new releases from myself and other Alkira Publishing authors, please sign up to the Alkira Publishing email list. In return you'll get a free ebook by an Alkira Publishing author. You'll find the sign-up button on the right-hand side under the photo at www.alkirapublishing. com. Of course, your information will never be shared, and the publisher won't inundate you with emails, just let you know of new releases.

And do take a look at my other book on writing, *The Elements of Active Prose: Writing Tips to Make Your Prose Shine*, available at all major online bookstores.

About the Author

Tahlia Newland is an editor, author, artist, and publisher who helps writers shape their books into a publishable product of which they can be proud. She is the managing editor at Alkira Publishing and brings decades of experience in the creative arts and contemplative practice to her editorial practice, offering a rare blend of technical precision and intuitive insight. Her editorial work is rooted in deep listening that honours each author's voice. With a Copy Editing and Proofreading Certificate from AOC (Australia) and a NZ Trained Teachers Certificate, Tahlia teaches her authors to write well and supports them at all stages of their writing journey.

Tahlia is the author of seven magical realism novels and several non-fiction books - on writing, meditation, and spiritual-abuse recovery. Her fiction explores metaphysical themes through lyrical, minimalist storytelling, while her non-fiction offers grounded tools for healing and creative growth. Before entering the publishing world, she spent twenty years in theatre in education and five years teaching high school creative and performing arts.

Beyond the page, she is a decorative and introspective artist, and a permaculture and meditation practitioner, who lives in an Australian rainforest with her husband and two Burmese cats.

http://tahlianewland.com

www.ingramcontent.com/pod-product-compliance
Lightning Source LLC
Chambersburg PA
CBHW032047020426
42335CB00011B/221